MW00413153

"Gail Larkin has achieved two brave things in her book that most EMS/fire professionals think about but do not bring to fruition in their lifetime—she provides a searingly honest portrayal of what we do as servant leaders; and, through her deep revelations, she leaves a legacy for the next generation to ponder. Past all the training and education, the darkness and despair, there are moments that give us hope in the humanity we all have inside us and for the human condition. It is through this journey that Ms. Larkin's writing reminds me of the old Greek proverb: *A society grows great when old men plant trees whose shade they know they will never sit in.* Through her sense of what is real, she's planting trees for public safety professionals to come, but this is a book for *anyone* who wants to understand what those in EMS deal with on a day-to-day basis."

—*Dr. Chris Nollette, NRP, LP,*
Professor of Emergency Medical Service,
Moreno Valley College / Ben Clark Training Center,
Riverside Community College District, California.
President,
National Association of EMS Educators (NAEMSE)

"*What We Carry* is the spiritual journey of a New York City paramedic as she explores her calling and finds herself. Gail Larkin touchingly recalls patients she has cared for and shows that, every time we touch another person, we take on part of them. She affirms the dignity of all people, no matter who they are—and more importantly, *where* they are—in life. This is a great read for anyone who has been in healthcare or who wants an insider's view of Emergency Medical Services."

—*Marie C. Diglio, BA, EMTP; CIC.*
Executive Director of Operations,
Regional Emergency Medical Services
of New York City (NYC REMSCO)

WHAT WE CARRY

WHAT WE CARRY

A New York Paramedic's Story

GAIL LARKIN

Full Court Press
Englewood Cliffs, New Jersey

First Edition

Copyright © 2018 by Gail Larkin

Published in the United States of America
by Full Court Press, 601 Palisade Avenue
Englewood Cliffs, NJ 07632
fullcourtpressnj.com

ISBN 978-1-946989-17-8
Library of Congress Catalog No. 2018946516

Editing and book design by Barry Sheinkopf

*Author photo by Bill Brokaw of Brokaw Photography
(brokawphotography.com)*

To Prof. Barry Sheinkopf,
for telling me, so many years ago, "Ya just
gotta get out there and live."

To my parents, Abigail and James,
who tolerated and even encouraged
the wild rides of my life out there.

To my daughters, Cate and Sarah,
for bringing to my life perspective, depth,
meaning, and endless joy. . .and for listening
to my endless medic war stories.

And to all the EMTs and Paramedics
who have gone before me
and go alongside me now,
and for those yet to come.
There's no way around it;
this job will change you—
mostly for the better, if you allow it.

TABLE OF CONTENTS

INTRODUCTION

WHEN I WAS FIRST DRAWN into the prehospital emergency medical field over forty years ago, I was young and mostly unencumbered by the baggage we all accumulate.

I remember hearing a car crash when I was younger—much younger—long before I even thought about entering the field. The sound of tires screeching, metal groaning as it was dragged across pavement— that sound, and the imagined images and cries of the injured, startled me as it would anyone, but I suspected that there was something different about how I felt. There was a *pull*, as if I were being drawn by a great magnet towards the scene. Both fear and the blind energy that come with too much adrenalin had my pulse racing and my skin tingling with a need to *do some-*

thing. I just *had* to *be* there. With no idea of what to do, I remained on the periphery of the accident and watched, certain that *I* was supposed to be the one doing something.

Was that what they mean by "a calling"? I could never understand that simultaneous horror and compulsion to do something when a tragedy struck. At first I thought that everyone felt that way. Clearly, though, they don't. Many turn away from these horrors I have run to for so many years.

I'VE ALWAYS IMAGINED OUR COLLECTIVE, as well as our individual, lives as tapestries. That's not a new idea. Every person encountered, every experience lived, adds more color, more threads, to the tapestry.

It's my life, and I don't have the perspective from a distance, so, like most of us, I have no real idea of what this tapestry *is.* But I know that all of my patients, encounters with families, interactions with strangers on the street—all of it—has added innumerable shades, both bright and dismal, to it.

I'm beginning to feel the threads tighten as they become crowded with experience. But enough of metaphor. What I carry—what *we* carry—makes us who we are.

WHEN I WAS COMPILING THE STORIES for this book, I was concerned, not that I would run out of interesting ones, but that I would not ever stop. What would I include? What would I leave out? Did I recall with accuracy? Would someone challenge me and tell me that I was making it all up?

If nothing else, I've come to realize that we fill in the blanks as best we can. Someone may dispute what I have written, but in the end we all see the world though a unique lens. Our recollection is a conglomeration of what happened and what we believe did.

Of course, names have been changed—some to protect privacy, others because I just don't remember. Details may be recalled with accuracy in some stories while, in others, the blanks have been filled in with what I can, to the best of ability, reconstruct. The important parts—the details that changed my life, that I have thought about so frequently and for so long—are both real and true.

As you go through this collection, you will encounter a small portion of what I can recall as significant. Life-changing. Memorable. But there are hundreds, maybe thousands, more stories that have touched me in such profound ways as to alter the manner in which I live my life, even many years later.

What is most clear to me is that it is not the excitement of a call that makes it significant, or the glamour of saving a life, but the small things that stay with us and become what we carry. It's not always a burden of pain. It can be the burden asking, *Did I do enough?*

One of my homeless patients once reminded me that the only thing that matters is that we love and are loved. What is left in the end is simple and twofold: Each encounter with a patient or family has helped me become a better person, and that brings me to wonder, and to hope: Did I bring the same to them?

WHAT WE CARRY

What we carry inside
becomes our ballast,
making our burden weighty,
trodding a deep path underfoot.

What we carry
presses us down
keeps us grounded still.
The deep paths give sure footing
to those who follow.

STRAW FOR THE FIRE

B ARRY SQUEEZED HIS EYES SHUT as he always did when thinking of precise words. (It was 1975 and the last day of my first year as an English major at the local community college). That day his squinting served the double purpose of blocking out the late afternoon sun as he turned his face to the sky, waiting for the answer to come.

"Well, look. I'll tell ya," he said, dropping his head back down to us and opening his eyes. "If you wanna be a writer, ya gotta do three things." He grinned a not quite grin-grimace and took a deep drag on his cigarette. We were sitting cross-legged, facing him, on the grass outside the B building of the college. We waited.

Exhaling slowly, he squinted again, this time in response to the surge of blue smoke rising to his eyes. He said, "Ya gotta write. Every day." He put one finger up. "Ya gotta read. A lot. The Masters. Everything." His index and middle finger pointed like a peace sign at the afternoon wisps of clouds. "And third," he paused, raising his ring finger. "Ya just gotta get out there and live. I mean. . ." again he paused and smirked. "Do ya think Ernest Hemingway wrote *The Old Man and The Sea* by reading a damn travel brochure? And what about *For Whom The Bell Tolls?* He wrote that. . . ." Barry drew in deeply on his cigarette before twisting the stubby filter into the grass. "He wrote that because he was a goddamn journalist for the North American Newspaper Alliance. He didn't watch some movie. He lived this shit, for God's sake! Ya gotta get out there and live. Look at me! I can't even get tenure here. I'm a graduate of Berkeley, for Chrissake. I graduated in sixty-nine. That's six friggin' years ago. You guys are English majors. What are ya gonna do with that degree?" He pulled in his lower lip and looked at each one of us, nodding. "You have a lot to think about. Enjoy the summer."

It was early June. My first year was done. I walked the mile along the Staten Island Expressway service road to the train station to save the thirty-five cents in bus fare. As I walked, I was thinking about his parting words. Get out there and live. So far, I had lots of mediocre poetry and some song lyrics, mostly inspired by a broken long-term relationship that, at that point in my worldly nineteen years, amounted to an ex-boyfriend of barely two of them. Throw in a childhood of playing in the swamps and woodlands surrounded by a sparsely populated neighborhood, and I would find that my only straw for the fire, as Barry would say, referring to my current favorite poet, Theodore Roethke, was limited to a high school romance and my non-Thoreau wanderings in the woods. Hmm, I thought, watching my sandaled feet poke out from the long overalls as I walked, I gotta get out there and live!

"LARKIN! GO ON YOUR BREAK! Come back on time. Twenty minutes, not thirty!" Teresita, the front-end manager at the grocery store, pointed to the punch-in clock as I tossed my pink smock into the office. "On time, Larkin!"

"Yeeesss, Terrah-*Seeeta*!" I grinned and hurried out the door, but not before she rolled her eyes and laughed.

I checked my watch, synchronized to the punch-in clock, while waiting for the light to change. Seventeen minutes left! As soon as the light changed, I ran across the street to Dunkin' Donuts and settled onto a pink plastic stool, facing the parking lot. I was soaking the last half of my honey-dipped stick in my coffee when I saw the ambulance pull into the lot. Three uniformed emergency medical technicians climbed out, black work boots hitting the pavement in a We Are the Shit attitude.

One of them laid the police scanner on the counter, and all three sat across from me. I stared. Each one of them wore a clean white uniform shirt with the blue-and-orange New York State Emergency Medical Technician patch sewn just below the right shoulder; on the left sleeve there was a red and white VHRU Volunteer Ambulance Corps patch. The only woman in the group, a curly haired blonde probably about ten years older than me, smiled when she noticed me looking at the stethoscope draped around her neck.

I took it as my opening. "You guys are EMTs? You get your training here on Staten Island? Do you have to be an EMT to start working on the ambulance? How did you get started?"

The blonde laughed and answered, "You have to take the EMT course, and then you take the state exam. You can join the ambulance corps any time, though, and start out dispatching and fund-raising. As soon as you get certified, you can sign up for shifts. This unit is all volunteer."

"Where do I take the course?" I asked her.

"There's only one on Staten Island right now. It's at the Marine Hospital—the public health hospital near Bay Street. A class is probably starting in September if you're really interested," she said. "I can give you a number—"

"Hey! Gail!" Louie from the supermarket was buying a coffee at the counter. "Teresita is looking for you. You're like ten minutes late from break!"

I checked my watch. Twenty-seven minutes had passed since I bolted from the store. "Crap. *Crap!*" I looked back at the EMTs, feeling embarrassed. "I work across the street in the supermarket. I gotta go."

"Here." The blonde EMT handed me a napkin with a phone number written on it. "My name's Barbara. This is the number to call. Tell Richie that you spoke to me."

"Thanks!" I stuffed the napkin into my pocket as I ran back across the street to work.

"So guess what? I found a place to take the EMT course." I watched my boyfriend's face for the expected reaction. Having recently completed his army service, where he received medical training, he was already working as an EMT.

"Babe, you don't want to do that. It's not for you." He tilted his head the way he always did when he was acting like my guardian. He shook his head and then quietly added, "It's not a job that you should do."

"I'm doing it. It's great life experience. What? I just went to a whole year of college. An English major. For *what?* Even my writing professor is telling us that there's no use in college. He's got all these degrees, and they won't even make his job permanent. I'm *doing* this. And besides, it's only volunteer. It's not like it's a career or anything."

"SO YOU'RE ONE OF THE STUDENTS from Richie's class? You can put your jacket and bag in here. I'm Kevin. I'm the head nurse in the E.R." He turned and pointed to the small room behind the nurses' station. "That's our break room, so if you want coffee or anything. . .anyway, you can keep your stuff in there. You have your own stethoscope? Bandage scissors?"

"I do." I dug my stethoscope out of my bag and flung it around my neck. I slid my bandage scissors, still unused, into the leg pocket of my uniform pants.

I was nearly done with my EMT class. This was my first of two mandatory shifts in the hospital. I would need to ride a couple of shifts on the ambulance as part of my internship as well.

"Okay, so come on. Let's go see what we've got." He picked up a clipboard from the desk and turned to a row of patient beds. I followed.

"This is Eddie. Overdose. Barbiturates. Hey, Ed. This is Gail, a student here for the day. Mind if she hangs out and keeps an eye on you?" Kevin was speaking kindly to the young man whose stringy hair hung limp, sticking to his face. A thick rubber tube extended from his right nostril. Attached to the end was a huge syringe tinted black with thick liquid.

Eddie raised his hand in slow motion and gave a wave, then tried to push the hair away from the corner of his mouth, scrunching his nose to try to reposition the tube. "Yeah. Cool. How ya doin'?" He leaned forward slightly and started to extend his hand, then thought better of it and let it drop to his lap. Fish-belly white legs extended out from the hospital gown that barely covered his crotch. He reached down and pulled the gown as far as it could go, to the tops of his thighs.

"Here ya go." Kevin handed me a sheet. "Make a

decent man out of him." He grinned at Eddie. "We got ya covered, champ."

I unfolded the sheet and placed it across his lap, careful not to touch his body.

"Oh. One more thing you might need. Here." Kevin handed me a turquoise plastic dish. "This is an emesis basin. You know what that is?"

I nodded. "Sure. In case he vomits."

"Yeah. Well, he came in pretty soon after he took the pills. Was conscious and alert. He got thirty of ipecac, so his stomach is pretty much empty now. Too bad you weren't here for that. We found quite a few of the pills in his vomit. I'll show you later. So, the doc just gave him some activated charcoal." Kevin pointed to a tall, nearly empty cup of slushy black liquid. "It helps soak up the last bits of toxins out of his stomach, if there's anything left. He should be fine, but stay here with the basin just in case he's not done vomiting." Kevin moved on to a woman holding an ice pack against the head of a crying toddler.

I wasn't sure what to say to Eddie. I think I asked him if he was cold. He started to answer, but instead of words, he retched. And retched again. Then the explosion of watery black grit, everywhere. The emesis basin was speckled with the charcoal sludge.

My arms looked like someone had flung black mud at them, and then I felt something warm dripping past my right eye.

Kevin hurried back to Eddie. He looked at me, first up, then down, then up again. Pressing his lips together to suppress a smile, he said, "Better go get yourself cleaned up. Bathroom's over there." He pointed in the direction of the break room. "Plenty of paper towels in there."

I tried not to make eye contact with any of the other nurses as I rushed to the bathroom. One, her starched, capped head never moving up from her notes, raised her hand and pointed towards the bathroom.

"I PASSED. I PASSED!" The wooden door slammed behind me as the rest of the mail slid across the gray Formica kitchen table. Waving my test results sheet in the air, I danced into the living room, where my two younger brothers were building booby traps with string, Hot Wheels tracks, and tape. I ducked around plastic superheroes dangling from the suspended tracks, extending from the Christmas tree to the coffee table. I held out the paper. "Check. This. Out!" I showed them the paper with my EMT card attached at the bottom. My brothers, ten and twelve years old, laughed, looked at each other, and shrugged. The dog ran circles around my legs.

I signed my card and carefully slid it into my wallet. "I gotta go buy some patches for my uniform!"

I yanked the door of my '66 Oldsmobile Cutlass open and slid across the cold vinyl seat. The engine started on the third try. I scraped ice off the inside of the windshield with my thumbnail and a spatula, and then drove the snowy roads to the uniform store.

"THIS IS YOUR FIRST SHIFT?" Bill asked. I was relieved to see that he, one of my skills instructors from class, was part of the crew on my first tour with the volunteer ambulance corps. He had the jump kit opened and was going through supplies, matching each item to the check list attached to a metal clipboard.

"Yep. Very first. I'm so psyched for this." I checked again to make sure I had penlight, stethoscope, bandage scissors. "Who else is on?" I watched as he reached into a cabinet above the stretcher and grabbed a stack of sterile gauze, which he added to the small stack in the side pocket of the jump kit.

"Richie." He smiled.

"Richie the instructor? From class?" My anxiety level notched up drastically.

Before he could answer, Richie's bellow sounded from the open front door. "Howdy. Let's go. We got one already. Pedestrian struck in the Grants shopping plaza parking lot."

Bill zipped the jump kit closed, wedged it under the end of the stretcher, and climbed through to the passenger seat in front.

The van rocked from side to side as Richie steered through traffic. *What's the ETA on the bus?* A voice crackled over the police radio. *Never mind. I see them.*

I heard Bill tell Richie, "Over there. Cops waving. There."

The ambulance took a sharp turn, accelerated, then stopped abruptly. I could hear people yelling.

"Grab the bag. Hand me the oxygen tank. Let's go!" Bill had the side door open already. Richie was pulling the wooden backboard out of the tall outside cabinet. He took long, fast strides toward the crowd.

A cop, with outstretched arms, stood with his back to a crowd of about fifteen people, yelling over his shoulder, "C'mon. *C'mon.* Move back. Let them through!" Most of them had their hands pushed into jacket pockets. A few had their arms across their chests. One woman had covered her mouth with her white furry-mittened hand. I quickly looked away when her eyes met mine.

Bill motioned for me. "Gail, take the head." I knelt down on the cold pavement. Slush soaked through the knees of my uniform pants, and I held the woman's head in line with the rest of her body. A white shopping bag was on the ground next to her. A red sweater stuck out of the bag. *Probably winter sale.* I thought momentarily of my mother, who loved sales and shopping. I quickly shook the image from my head.

Her eyes were open, staring up at me. Bill was cutting her coat and covering her in a blanket at the same time. "Can you hear me? What's your name?" The woman didn't speak. I caught a glimpse of a tire track across her swollen belly.

Richie tossed the hissing oxygen mask in my direction. I carefully pulled the elastic around the woman's head and adjusted the mask across her nose and mouth.

I wondered if she could feel my hands shaking as I continued holding her head. "Just don't move. We're going to get you to the hospital in a few minutes." I couldn't tell if she understood what I was telling her. She blinked and just kept staring.

"Okay. Let's move. On the head count. Roll her onto the board. Ready?" Richie spoke in my direction.

"Huh? Oh, okay. Um. On three. One. Two. Three." We rolled her carefully and propped the board behind her.

"Okay. Back on three. One. Two. Three." Definitely not like the classroom, I thought. We finished securing her and rolled the stretcher to the ambulance.

AFTER EVERY AMBULANCE CORPS meeting for the next three years, I rushed to the sign-up table and penciled my name into every Wednesday and Saturday night shift for the month. Although the shift was supposed to be 7:00 p.m. until midnight, I had a regular crew by then, one that often included either Mike, EMT-firefighter boyfriend at the time, or my sister, Debby, and we almost always stayed out—especially on Saturday nights—until 5:00 a.m. We all wanted to be there for the "good calls."

On one particularly foggy summer night, we were driving slowly, unable to see even a car length ahead of us. The police scanner crackled with call after call.

We responded to a collision with injuries. The dispatcher reported a car overturned in a ditch near the ball field.

I knew the area; it wasn't far from my house. Although the officers on scene were calling for a rush, we crawled along the road, trying to stay close to the median and hoping no other cars would hit us.

The police car was barely visible through the fog, although the officers had left their flashing beacons on. We scrambled down the embankment and found the car, overturned, with the back windshield shattered.

"The driver's inside," Artie, the cop closest to the car, told us. We nodded and carefully climbed over rocks and weeds to the driver's side. "She's conscious. I don't know if she's hurt. Lucky she's alive. Look at this thing. You're not gonna get at her from that side. Gotta try going around the back," he said, pointing to the shattered rear window.

Squatting down on the mucky ground, I could see her inside the car. "Don't move, ma'am. *Don't move.*"

"Okay, so let's get going. How we gonna get her out?" Mike had asked the question that most of us were thinking. Resources were scarce. Every unit was on other assignments. Even Fire Rescue had a delayed response. Mike wedged the backboard under the car, and I started to crawl onto it before anyone could argue.

"I'll go in," I said, lying flat on the board. I did a combat crawl along it and through the back windshield towards the woman. Luckily the roof hadn't caved in, and the car seemed stable enough. She was half-sprawled on her back across the back seat. Her legs were still hooked over the front seat. Wrapping my hands under her shoulders, I cradled her head between my elbows. "Okay. Let us move you. Just relax. We're going to get you out."

"Okay, okay." Her voice was barely a whisper.

I bent my torso sideways as much as I could so they would hear my shouts. "Pull me out by my feet! I got her!" I felt strong hands grip above my boots. I started moving backwards a little at a time. As I moved, I hung on to the woman, keeping my arms under her armpits, my hands gripping her shirt at the shoulders. She slowly slid onto the board. I wriggled the rest of the way out, over the slimy ground, brushing bits of glass from my muddy clothes.

Once out, the rest of the crew secured her, checked her over, and lifted her into the ambulance. The fog, still blindingly white, obscured the road as we made our way slowly to the hospital. It wasn't until we climbed back in to the ambulance after leaving the hospital that the fog began to thin. The sunrise was a distant, hazy orb when we finished our shift and headed home.

"So why do you want to be a Corpsman?" The Human Resources director for the New York City Emergency Medical Services (then run by Health and Hospitals Corporation) leaned forward in his folding chair, tucking his dark green tie into his shirt.

"I just think it's a great job. I've been working on a volunteer unit for three years, and I really like it. I want to do this as my career."

He was silent. Staring. "Well, this isn't a great job for girls. There's lifting. And we can place you anywhere in the city. It's tough out there. Not everything is like Staten Island. *That's* the country club. You'll have to be okay with working shifts. And you can't pick your partner. You have to be able to *pull your weight*." He leaned forward and delivered the last part with a sneer.

I thought, *He* probably can't lift—sitting in his office all day. I smiled. "I can lift."

"Fine. There's a physical. Let's see if you pass."

He handed me a slip of paper with a date on it. "Next week. If you pass, you'll have your driving test soon after. Good luck."

"Thanks. I'll pass," I said.

FOUR WEEKS LATER, I STOOD in my kitchen and read the notice out loud. "'Congratulations on becoming a New York City Corpsman.' Yes!"

It was 1978, and New York City Emergency Medical Services still operated as a paramilitary organization. You were either a motor vehicle operator (MVO), a corpsman, or a paramedic, regardless of gender.

It would be a few more years before they officially changed the title from 'corpsman' to 'EMT'. But by then I was a paramedic and had worked in a few different parts of the city—days, evenings, and nights. Death had become familiar, and the saves were few but memorable. Most of the time there was no follow-up. We either saved someone, or we didn't.

MARTY WAS ONE OF THE FORTUNATE for whom our efforts had a nice, life-saving sort of effect! I had nearly forgotten him until a woman, approaching the ambulance, reminded me.

Her gloved hand was gripping a Dunkin' Donuts bag, and the bottom of her wool coat flapped in the bitterly cold breeze, exposing her knees. Glancing up at us after maneuvering around a frozen puddle, she moved slowly across the parking lot.

"I think she's coming this way," my partner, Louie, moaned. "Shit. I just want to have my damn coffee in peace. People need to just leave us alone."

The gloved hand tapped on the window. I rolled it down. Her words came out in quick clouds. "You're the people that saved my husband. You were at my house last week!" She smiled, and her crimson-lip-sticked lips stretched across her face. "I wanted to say thank you. Here." She smiled and lifted the bag through the open window. "Jelly donuts!"

I stared at her face, wispy gray hair curling up and around a thick magenta scarf. Blinking with watery eyes, she grabbed at the scarf and held it tightly against the wind. "It was Marty. My Marty. You revived him. He's coming home tomorrow!" She looked at me, waiting for recognition.

"Oh, Marty! Of course! He's coming home? That's great." I did remember him. I decided that Marty's wife looked considerably better than she had the week before, when Marty nearly checked out.

Breathless in the cold, she continued, "I didn't know how to thank you, and then I saw you sitting here and just wanted to say thank you, and, well, I bought you both some donuts."

My partner, in his usual snide way, mumbled something about jelly donuts and how he hoped she wasn't bringing any to Marty. Without turning around I swung my hand up to shush him.

I'm pretty sure that Marty's wife meant it to be a compliment—a bag of jelly donuts—*and I hope they're the raspberry ones*—as a reward for keeping her Marty on the planet a while longer.

"I'm on my way there now to see him. Thank you so much!" I watched her furry boots step precariously around the ice and back to her car.

Marty. Huh. So he lives. Luckily for Marty, his heart stopped at the same time that I was taking his pulse. Just like that. Flat on his back on the floor of a very narrow hallway, right outside his bathroom in a nice two-bedroom ranch. I had to keep one leg out straight and lean over his chest sideways to deliver the compressions. Most people think just like the TV taught them to—do CPR, save a life. If they only knew that most people who drop dead just like that don't survive, CPR or not. But as I said,

Marty's heart stopped right in the middle of me counting his pulse. His wife told us that he was on his way to the bathroom, dropped in the hall, and stared off without responding. Her ten-year-old grandson called 9-1-1. So we arrived and found him where he had fallen.

"He's not responding. He's breathing, though. Let's get some oxygen on him. He has a pulse. It's pretty irregular, and I can only feel it at his carotid." My fingertips pressed into the groove between the muscles in his neck and his windpipe. As I was counting the pulse, it disappeared. Just like that. There wasn't even room to kneel at his side, so, as I mentioned, I awkwardly started compressions leaning alongside him.

"We need to move him. I can't work like this. We gotta get him out to the living room. Ma'am, please take your grandchildren out of the living room and maybe put them in one of the bedrooms. We need to work on him. We'll be here for awhile."

"What's going on? What happened? He was just talking to me. Oh, my God. Please save him. What's going on?" Marty's wife looked confused. Her voice became more shrill with each word.

"Right now we're helping his heart pump blood to

his brain. We're doing everything that would normally be done in the emergency room, so there's no time wasted. Does he take any medicine?"

"Yes, I mean, he's supposed to. He never takes it on time. His doctor told him—"

"Maybe you could go get his meds. Put all the bottles in a bag for us, so we can take them with us," I told her.

One hand over her mouth and the other hand sliding across the paneled wall to steady herself, she took short fast steps to the kitchen.

"Okay, let's get him out there where we have more room. Ready. On three. One, two, three." We grabbed his feet and dragged him into the living room; the pungent odor of feces rose as his bowels emptied into his khakis.

"He shit himself." I glanced up in the direction of the comment. A police officer, not more than twenty-three years old, looked down at Marty's still body. The officer pulled his lips tight in an effort to block the stench.

"Excuse me?" I looked at him and hoped Marty's wife was busy elsewhere. The rookie looked at me and raised his eyebrows, speaking more slowly this time. "He shit himself. That usually means they're gone, right? I mean, this guy just let it loose. He's dead, right?"

I looked up at him again, while counting off chest compressions. "You-guys-take-CPR-at-the-Academy,-right?"

"Ugh, yeah but we don't really use it. It's just a part of, of—"

"Okay, get down over here, on this side. Here's your chance. I need you to do the compressions while my partner gets the EKG paddles charged. We have to get a tube into his lungs, get an IV into him, push some meds, get things rolling."

"I'm not really—I mean, I never did CPR. Don't you have another unit coming?"

"There's no time to wait. We're busy today. The weather, the roads are bad. Everybody's calling 9-1-1," I told him. He was, by then, definitely paler.

He knelt down across from me, Marty unresponsive between us. "Here, watch. Use the heel of your hand. It's not rocket science. Just place your hands here, yeah. Like that. Good. Move your knees close to his chest and just bend from your waist. That's it. See? You're a natural. A little faster. It's one and two and three and. . .that's it. Okay, just keep going. In a few minutes, he'll have a tube going into his lungs, so you won't even have to stop while my partner ventilates him," I said.

The rookie's leather belt, still new and stiff, squeaked with each bend as he rocked over Marty's chest. Gagging, his head moved forward, and his hat toppled to the floor. I tossed it off to the side. "How long do I do this for?" he asked

"Just keep going. We'll let you know."

Shortly after, Marty began to moan. The rest, as you know, is jelly donut history.

"PROFESSOR LARKIN, HOW LONG have you been a medic?" Dan, my twenty-two-year-old paramedic student, challenged me to answer.

"Well, let's see. I became an EMT first. . .hmmm. Ford was president." I smiled.

"Who?" Kristina, who's from Uzbekistan, had no idea.

Another student answered, "Wasn't he, like, president back in the eighties?"

"Ohhh. Seventies," I mumbled. And added, a bit louder, *The nineteen-seventies.* That was a year. Before you were born. Probably before your parents were born."

Alexandra laughed. "I think my grandmother was

born back then."

"Oh. Goody," I said jokingly. "Maybe I delivered her." I rolled my eyes. "Okay. So let's get started on the lesson, shall we?"

"Tell us some war stories!" Peter, the oldest student at thirty-one, laughed.

"Did you always want to be a paramedic?" Dan is determined to get more answers.

"No. Actually, I started out as an English major," I said. "I'll tell you about it some time."

WHEN I DECIDED TO FINALLY go back and finish my degree in the mid-1990s, I went back to the community college where I started in 1974. I was surprised to see Barry Sheinkopf still listed in the catalog as an English professor. He remembered me, and we chatted for a short time. He told me about a school he had opened in New Jersey.

"Ya gotta come by sometime and check it out. It's The Writing Center. A load of fun. We get all sorts of writers. Nice little place. It's in the basement of a real estate office. We got it set up real nice." Barry smiled his usual smirky grin and nodded, probably knowing that I wouldn't be showing up at his place any time soon.

It was 1995, and I was busy raising my daughters, soon to be trying to find my way out of a flailing marriage.

I stored the information about Barry's writing center deep into my memory.

"So, Professor Larkin, what kind of stuff do you write?" The questions from my paramedic students persisted.

"Mostly medical and technical. But I'd really like to write more creative stuff."

I drove home that night thinking about how fast the decades had slipped by. Wow. Nearly forty years since I took my EMT class. And even longer since I left college to "get out there and live."

I googled *The Writing Center* and, before going to bed that night, I wrote a brief email to Barry.

I'm not sure if you remember me. I was hoping to take one of your writing workshops. Is that possible?

I had my answer the next morning.

In January 2015, I drove the thirty-five miles to the Center and parked in the small lot behind the building.

I entered and crept quietly down the stairs. I heard a familiar voice singing a Gordon Lightfoot song. Rhythmic guitar picking that I would know anywhere accompanied Barry's voice. I hadn't heard him sing in decades.

Five other students sat with us around a large wooden table in a paneled basement. Barry's photographs covered the walls. I scanned the books on a shelf: Auden, Angelou, and some of Barry's own books.

We went around the room and introduced ourselves. I was the only newcomer. "Hi. I'm Gail. I'm here to get better at writing, something I've wanted my whole life and finally decided to just do it." I paused, heads nodded, some warm smiles welcomed me. "Actually, forty-plus years ago I was in a few of Barry's classes at the College of Staten Island. He was a popular professor, and we often stayed later than scheduled to hear his words of wisdom which changed the course of my life."

I PROBABLY DIDN'T WRITE ENOUGH, nor did I read the Masters enough. But I did get out there and "live."

In 1974, Barry turned us on to Theodore Roethke's *Straw for the Fire*. Now, decades later, I'd found my way back—finally, this time with something to write about.

> *What goes before me? Myself alone;*
> *What lives again? Only a man of straw—*
> *Yet straw can feed a fire to melt down stone.*
> *—Theodore Roethke*

GENTLE NOW

THE ONE I REMEMBER MOST was when I was still a newly hired EMT working for New York City EMS, stationed in Queens. The call came over as an "unconscious male" in a basement apartment. We followed police officers into the apartment—dark and damp. We found our patient.

He had hanged himself from the inside of his bathroom door. The dirty blue terrycloth bathrobe belt was tight around his neck and tied somehow to the top of the door. How, I don't recall. What I do recall—as in other 911 calls where our patient's life was lost at his or her own hands—is the thickness of the air, the dark gray despair that was like a shroud that engulfed me, a toxic pair of desperate arms inviting me to feel pain and helplessness.

He was a frail, elderly man. Small brown eyes still open, thin hair more than past due for a shampoo and trim. Out of duty and habit, I touched the groove between his windpipe and neck muscle, knowing I wouldn't find a pulse. His skin was cold, rubbery, empty of all human warmth.

Briefly, I wondered whether the robe belt had been part of a gift from some holiday or birthday long past.

The landlord had called 911 after his tenant's mail piled up for a few days. There were no pets, no decorations or photos: The furniture was sparse. A small metal table and a couple of mismatched chairs occupied a tiny kitchenette space. It had taken us only a few seconds to walk the length of the entire apartment, from his entryway to the bathroom, where he was hanging.

I couldn't allow myself to think too much about him in those early days of my career. It's been close to forty years, and small chunks of memory work their way to the surface now and then, not unlike the tiny shards of glass from childhood falls that the body eventually pushes through the skin.

Doing my job well often meant pushing away emotion—well, not really *away*, but down to where it would stay hidden like a time capsule in the soil, forgotten until some random movement stirred the ground far in the future.

From this distance, I can see that all the emotions that we put away without ever feeling them become like great pieces of ice against our soul, numbing us to feeling anything but the most muted of emotions, colorless, tasteless, like carbon monoxide with its quiet but persistent toxicity clinging to our blood. Stoic living slowly kills us.

And from this distance I can, at last, feel his sadness and allow myself to feel my own as well.

Dylan Thomas tells us, *Do not go gentle into that good night.*

But what happens when the nights—too many of them strung together like broken beads—no longer qualify as good? What is the human soul to endure through sad, long, lonely ones, over and over? Where is the purpose of struggle when no change is possible? When all hope is lost, the darkness comes. It erases the light of joy and memories of family. And of love. How could he have broken through such a profound thing?

He did not rage against the dying of the light, and that is what still makes me sad. But feeling it opens the path again to hope that someone now holds his spirit gently, as I hold his memory.

WHAT WE CARRY

ABE GUNNED THE ENGINE as soon as his line of vision at the intersection was clear. My head slammed back into the headrest of the seat, and we quickly gained speed along the nearly empty road.

"Hey, Abe! What the. . . !" I grabbed the *Oh, Shit* handle above the door. "What's the rush? It's an accident. Probably unfounded."

Our call had come in moments earlier as an MVA, a motor vehicle accident with unknown injuries. On that sparsely traveled piece of road this late at night, it was either nothing or a mess.

Before Abe had a chance to defend his lightning response time—since he was usually deliberate and careful responding to calls—the dispatcher's voice came through. *PD says put a rush on it. Numerous calls. Confirmed overturned.*

My heart rate cranked up several notches. We rounded a sharp curve. The red flashing lights ahead blinded me for a second until my eyes adjusted.

It was a mess.

Cops had already closed off the road, so we parked in the middle of the boulevard. A few miles north, we would have been surrounded by restaurants and bars— the local kind. That stretch was just medical offices flanked by older homes in a mostly dark and quiet neighborhood.

But that was quickly changing. Already, people in bathrobes, tee shirts, and sweats were gathering on the sidewalk.

I make it my thing to try to avoid making eye contact with bystanders. That night was no exception. I kept my head down and my eyes focused on the horror in front of me.

What was left of a red convertible—maybe a Mustang? A Charger? Did they come in convertible?— chunks of twisted metal, was scattered on the roadway stretching out behind the car. The engine was still running. I could see a young man hanging upside down from the front passenger seat.

"Hey, Rizzo! Anyone else around?" I wondered who'd been driving before the car flipped.

Angelo Rizzo was a cop who was two years from retirement. At a distance, his long, lean frame would've placed him in the thirty-something category. Up close, he had the earned lines of street years on his tanned face and just the beginning of gray at the temples in a full head of otherwise black hair. His ocean-blue Sicilian eyes had the attention of most of the nurses in the ER. And the female paramedics—well, there was only one, me—but yeah. Rizzo.

"Baby girl, you don't wanna see. They're done. There's three other kids besides this one, but they're gone. Pieces scattered all over."

Abe turned toward me, tossing the trauma bag. In his usual protective way, he said, "Here, you take this one. I'll check the others."

Squeezing under the edge of the car, I could hear snoring and gurgling coming from the kid who was dangling—apparently the only one who had been wearing a seat belt on impact. And the only one who'd survived. Barely.

I reached over to his still body and pressed the tips of my fingers against his neck to check a pulse. It was weak and rapid. Blood was hanging in a half-congealed stream from his mouth. *At least his airway is draining in this position,* I thought. "I have no idea how the hell I'm going to get him out of here without making things worse," I said out loud. I couldn't reach the seat belt buckle. It was lost in the tangle of sharp metal that trapped his body.

Then I felt a hand grab my ankle.

"You gotta get out. We're gonna turn the car over. You gotta move!" The fire department had arrived. I backed out, crouched low on all fours. Seven firefighters were impatiently waiting for me to get out of the way.

"The kid—I have to hang on to him. You can't just flip the car. If he's got broken bones, a neck injury—"

"We gotta do this *now*." The booming voice from under a black-and-yellow helmet was persistent. I had no better solution, so I stood up and stepped aside.

They had the car upright in seconds. Pebbled windshield glass and grit crunched underfoot as I rushed over to climb inside the crushed car and extricate the kid. Rizzo was climbing into the driver's seat to check him for ID.

The unresponsive teen's face and head were covered in slippery blood. I had to grip his hair to get his head up and airway open.

"Here," I told one of the firefighters. "Take his head like this while I get the backboard. We gotta get him into the ambulance and to the hospital, like *right now*." He did, while I checked for other injuries. We guided the kid onto a long backboard, secured him, and then hurried to the ambulance.

Once inside, I hit the overhead lights. Bright light. Cut and cover. My shears sliced away his Levis and laces. As I cut, I examined, then covered, his torso with a sheet to maintain body heat.

Brand new Pumas. My brother just bought Pumas. Stop thinking! Act! I forced myself to keep moving quickly and not think about it in any personal way. *High school ring.* I paused and turned it to see the date. He had just graduated last month. *No! Stop!* He could have been my brother. *He's not! Stop it!*

Oxygen on. Intravenous in. Large-bore IV with fluids running in. Blood pressure dropping. Clearly, he had internal bleeding as well as a massive head injury. I was torn between replacing his lost blood and being careful not to increase his pressure too much, for fear of making the pressure in his head worse.

Rizzo opened the back door. "Memorial?"

"Yeah. Give us an escort?" I shook my head,

silently indicating that the kid was probably not going to make it.

"Kevin Matthews. Seventeen. His ID says he lives two blocks from here," Rizzo said, and he seemed to know what I was thinking.

"Two blocks?" I leaned forward to glance out of the small window at the crowd gathered on the sidewalk and wondered if the kid's parents were among the bystanders. I prayed that they weren't. "Shit." I closed my eyes for a moment and then, looking at Rizzo, said, "Let's go. . .Abe, you're calling this in? We need a surgical standby."

"I got it already," he said solemnly, and we lurched forward. I pushed away the thoughts of the phone call to the Matthews family.

THE BRAIN IS A STRANGE ORGAN. It holds our thoughts. Gives us fear. Helps us overcome that fear. Keeps us alive and sometimes causes us to lose our life.

Kevin had massive brain injury. I couldn't see it directly, but I watched him carefully as we raced through the darkness of the road ahead. His pupils became fixed and dilated. His brain was bleeding. A strong skull, the same one that protected him from falls as he learned to walk, and from injury from collisions during football practice, was trapping the blood inside. The impact with the roadway and whatever else he slammed against on impact had thrown too much force against the arteries in his brain, and they had ruptured and bled. And his skull was still intact, allowing the blood to build up a great and awful pressure inside his cranial vault, squeezing his brainstem through the same opening at the base of his skull that his spinal cord went through to carry impulses to his body. I watched, helpless, as his breathing became erratic and his arms bent upward and towards his chest. Decorticate posturing—a sign of increased pressure inside the brain; and then his arms extended down at his sides; an even surer indication that his brain was herniating. It was being squeezed out of his skull and down into the opening made only for a spinal cord. He had serious injuries to his internal organs as well, but the head injury. . . .

By the time we made the six-minute trip to the emergency department, Kevin Matthews would be brain dead.

HIS PARENTS WERE SITTING in the waiting area as I left the emergency department. My eyes very briefly locked with his mother's, and I turned away in shame, but not before I saw her gaze drop to my blood-soaked shirt. She knew, as only a parent could know, that I was wearing her son's blood, like a scarlet letter, on my white uniform shirt. I couldn't save him. I felt worthless, ashamed. I had done nothing wrong, but I had her son's blood all over me. I was going home. My brothers were alive, home, watching some silly late-night television show.

I would have already changed into clean clothes by the time I got there. But still, I would carry Kevin's invisible blood into my home, into my living room where my seventeen-year-old brother and my fifteen-year-old brother were stretched out on the worn rug. They would be laughing at the TV screen in recently deepened voices, the dog curled up between them. I'd fix them both big bowls of chocolate chip mint ice cream. They'd grab the dishes with their adult-like hands, look at me with a curious kind of head tilt, and ask me how my night had been.

And I would tell them it was okay, a few calls, and watch them eat their ice cream and let the television sound fill the empty spaces.

THE WHEELS
ON THE BUS

THE MIDDLE-AGED WOMAN was standing at the top of a brick stairway leading to the front door of a semi-attached home. Carl, one of my regular partners on the three-to-eleven shift on the only paramedic (ALS) ambulance on Staten Island at that time, climbed the stairs ahead of me.

I was just crossing the living room when he simultaneously said, "Oh! Okay," and picked up his pace. He had a year on me in medic seniority, and although I was relatively new, I already recognized some of his moves that meant *This is bad.* He had spotted the patient seconds before me and hurried into the kitchen.

I followed, and immediately saw the reason for his

notched-up focus.

Our patient looked to be about sixty years old. He was pale and sweating profusely, staring at us in great expectation that we would help him.

We moved quickly—getting vital signs, listening to his lungs, administering oxygen, obtaining a history. In just a few moments we had him strapped in to the stair chair and were making our way to the ambulance.

By the time we rolled off to the hospital a few minutes later, he had an intravenous line running, medication, and a heart monitor attached.

It was 1979, and there were no cardiac catheterization labs on standby back then. In fact, emergency treatment of blocked coronary arteries and heart attack was still in its early stages, though most medical professionals could easily recognize a major heart attack. This was one of those times.

I hopped into the driver's seat and radioed the dispatcher, requesting a notification at the closest hospital equipped to handle this sort of emergency. We had at least a twelve-minute ETA.

I pushed the accelerator once we hit the highway. It was nearing rush hour, so we maxed our speed at about fifty-five. That was our first lucky break—not that we would have driven too much faster, maybe sixty or so, if traffic had been light. The next bit of luck came from the fact that we were driving on the Staten Island Expressway, left lane, right alongside a very wide grassy median.

A FEW MINUTES FROM OUR EXIT, I felt a sudden jolt, and the ambulance took a hard lean to the left. Something large flew past the window—a tire! It bounced along the roadway for a second and then sailed across the grassy median.

Carl's head popped through the small opening from the patient compartment. "What the hell! What happened?"

I feathered the brakes quickly and caught a glimpse of the surprise and confusion on his face.

Keeping my voice at a whisper, I said, "We lost our wheel."

At that moment, the second wheel from the tandem pair lost its grip on the axle. It sailed past us, and that, too, bounced to the left, onto the grassy median and out of sight. Glancing in the side-view mirror, I watched sparks fly from the axle that was dragging on the roadway.

"Pull over! Pull over!" Carl hissed quietly.

The axle screeched and thumped along the pavement.

"I *am!*" I continued decelerating while trying to move to the right lane. "I gotta slow it down first!"

"What's happening? What's that noise?" Our patient knew something was up.

Carl's head disappeared, and I heard his voice, louder now, from the patient compartment. "It's okay, sir. Everything's fine. We just have a slight mechanical problem. No big deal. We'll have to have another ambulance meet us. Should be here in a few minutes."

I grabbed the microphone and explained quickly and very quietly to the dispatcher, "We have a cardiac patient—our vehicle is broken down. We need a backup right away. We're eastbound on the Staten Island Expressway, right before the Clove Road exit."

Lucky break number three. Another unit was nearby and met us within minutes.

We held our fingers to our lips as they gawked at the tireless left rear of the ambulance. We couldn't risk any more stress to our patient.

The unit backed up towards us, rear door to rear door. We took their stretcher out and rolled ours, with the patient still comfortably strapped in, right into the other ambulance.

Carl rode with our patient. I stayed with the vehicle, waiting for the tow truck.

The fourth and fifth lucky break had been that no one was hit by the bouncing, flying tires, and that our patient made it to the hospital without any complications.

Sometimes things can go horribly wrong in life; but at others, they go *wonderfully* right.

LEADER

THE JANUARY WIND STUNG MY EYES, and I blinked in the late afternoon sun. It was day eight of a cold spell. Even dressed in warm layers, I couldn't get used to the blast of winter each time I left the heated ambulance cab.

Frank and I hurried to the glass door of the office building. I yanked it open and felt the rush of warmth as we entered, took a deep breath, and blew out a sigh of relief, but not before my eyes stung again—not at the biting wind, but at the sour stench of feces and rotting flesh.

SUCH ODORS, AND THEIR SOURCES, were not uncommon in the Lower East Side, where we worked. We were fortunate, though, to have a supervisor who set the bar pretty high for his crews. We knew he would back us up no matter what. And for that, we always tried to do the right thing. It was just the way it was back then. We knew we had a good thing going. We were treated with respect, and, in turn, treated others, even the most difficult of patients, with respect. Tony, our boss, led by example. We went to work because we wanted to. And if any of us had a particularly bad night or needed what Tony referred to as a "mental health day," we could call in sick with no excuses—as long as someone was willing to cover our shift. We didn't abuse the privilege, but, knowing we had that option made the difficult calls a lot more tolerable.

A building security guard pointed us to the source of the smell. A man of indeterminate age was sitting on a low wall surrounding a small decorative fountain. With shaking arms, he tried to push himself to a standing position. "Sir," I called out, "stay right there. We'll check you out first."

"You're gonna take him, aren't you?" The security guard's voice was close to panic. "He can't stay *here!*"

Frank opened the stair chair and covered it with an open blanket while giving the guard a slow sideways look. "Yeah. He's. . .what's your name?

William? Okay. Yeah. William's coming with us."

We did our initial survey on him to rule out any immediately life-threatening concerns and found him surprisingly alert and stable, but he probably wouldn't have survived another night on the street.

"I only came in here to warm up," he said quietly as he held up his hands.

I reached for them and carefully pulled back the too-long sweatshirt sleeves. My stomach jumped. His fingertips were blackened and had open, pustulent sores. Large blisters covered the rest of the fingers and parts of both palms. I had never seen a worse case of deep frostbite. I gently placed sterile gauze pads between each of the fingers and winced as I watched him silently cry. I knew that the blackened fingertips were likely numb and necrotic, but the rest of the hands, judging by his response, must have been horribly painful.

We removed his shoes and socks once inside the warm ambulance. His feet were even more swollen and blistered than his hands and stank of dying tissue. I bandaged his feet loosely, like his hands. His pain seemed just a notch less when the bandaging was finished.

I gathered more of his information as we made our

way back to Cabrini. "Have you been on the street all week?" I couldn't imagine how he had survived the sub-freezing temperatures. It had been one of those weeks when police officers were ordered to get everyone off the streets and into a shelter. No doubt our patient had a few good hideouts, risking life and limb in the cold rather than in the crowded and potentially violent environment of a shelter.

For some homeless people, avoiding the mandatory street evacuation in a cold snap was simply an attempt not to be bussed out of Manhattan. Some of them had explained to me that it would be too difficult to get back home—even if home was just a park bench or doorway or subway stairway. Others had a long history of psychiatric illness and offered no explanation for why they preferred the street to a shelter.

William didn't talk much on the way in.

"When was the last time you ate anything?" I asked him.

He shrugged.

THE ER WAS, AS USUAL, busy when we arrived. A nurse stopped long enough to hear our brief history of our patient, then signed the ambulance call report. She wearily pointed to an empty bed. "Just put him over there."

It was close to dinnertime, and the steel cart rolled into the ER on schedule. The shelves of the cart contained trays of cellophane-wrapped sandwiches and covered Styrofoam bowls of soup.

I saw William looking at the cart.

I lifted one of the bowls. Small droplets of moisture clung to the plastic cover of the warm soup. "Can he have one of these?" I held up the soup for Violet, the head nurse, to see.

"He has no trouble breathing? No nausea?" she asked.

I shook my head.

"Sure."

With the patient privacy curtain mostly closed, I set up a small wheeled table next to William. The back of the ER bed was raised to a sitting position, and William, hands still bandaged and useless, slowly sipped spoonfuls of soup.

I heard Tony's voice. "Where's Larkin?" After a few seconds I could see his feet on the other side of the curtain. Whipping it back, he stared. I held the plastic soup spoon midway to William's mouth and waited.

He looked from the spoon, to William's hands, back to the spoon. Pressing his palm to his forehead, he shook his head but then nodded. "You guys are in service?" he asked. The dispatcher has you available?"

"Yep. Frank's in the bus. He knows I'm here."

Tony looked at William. "You okay, Chief?"

William nodded.

Tony looked back at me and then, looking up and waving his hand at the ceiling in feigned disbelief, he let go of the curtain and walked away.

He had taught us well.

William was just one of so many patients truly cared for by EMTs and paramedics who had the honor of working under Tony, a graduate of the first paramedic class in New York City.

Thirty-five years later, he's an emergency room physician, still reminding others that the patient always comes first.

FOREVER YOUNG

THE SUN WAS LOW ENOUGH behind the buildings to drag some of the thick July air with it, a small but steady trickle of evening cool from the East River meandering down Second Street. Thin metal folding chairs accommodating large bodies dotted the sidewalk like Monopoly pieces scattered on a game board. Dripping bottles of Corona were being drained into smiling mouths.

I leaned back in the cracked vinyl-covered seat of the ambulance, so I could stretch and rested my booted feet through the window opening on the door. My partner, Frank, was flossing his teeth, sucking in air after each pull through his molars.

"Do you really have to do that? It sounds disgusting."

"What? You floss your teeth in here all the time."

"Yeah, but I don't make those sucky sounds."

He thrust his torso across the console and at my face, his tongue pressed up against his teeth as he made exaggerated sucking noises.

"Oh, God. You. Are. Gross." Tossing my half-smoked cigarette out the window, I reached for my backpack and pulled out my stash of mint-flavored floss. As I sat up, someone outside bent quickly and picked up the still-lit cigarette. I recognized him as he inhaled deeply and approached the open window. "You threw out a good smoke, man." Smoke streamed through the spaces between his broken teeth. He grinned and nodded at Frank through the open window. Looking back at me, he said, "So what's cookin', good lookin'?"

"Gary, I would have given you a cigarette. You don't have to pick mine up off the sidewalk. Here."

"No, man. I don't wanna waste."

"Here. Take it for later."

A large muscular hand with long, yellowed, crusted nails took the unlit cigarette from me. With fingers more nimble than one would have expected, he tucked it behind an ear, pushing back greasy black hair with it.

"So, Gary, check this out. Someone broke the window of my car, stole my clothes. They weren't even new. I was gonna go to a party after work. They stole my damn *clothes.*"

He shook his head. "They steal everything. Probably get a few bucks. Nice clothes?"

"No. Just a plain cotton sweater. You know, like a summer thing. Just a top and some jeans."

"Yeah, but you know. It's survival, man. Sell that stuff here on the sidewalk. People buy anything. I don't break no windows. And I would never rip you off. You're a good lady. I make enough selling stuff I find."

I didn't have to ask him, Enough for what? Gary was a hundred-dollar-a-day junkie. A former carpenter, he'd hit it big working detail jobs in Laguna Beach. But California was just a dream for him now. For a few years he had ridden the crest of a wave he thought would never crash. Cocaine kept his fantasy ride alive a little longer until he started using, as he told the story, "Just a little dab of heroin to take the edge off." He'd told me that he didn't even remember how long it had taken. He lost his job. No one would hire a carpenter who was too high to see the mangling of his once-meticulous craftsmanship. His apartment and actress-wannabe girlfriend had disappeared with the California sunset, over the same horizon as his bank account.

Looking at him, I wondered if people ever really come back from their private journey into hell.

"I don't even care about the clothes, but what the hell, my window? That's expensive to fix, and I can't exactly park around the hospital with no glass in the window. Whatever."

He seemed to ponder this as he pinched the cigarette butt and squinted, getting two more short drags before he flicked it into the gutter.

I turned to Frank. "You want a coffee?"

"Yeah. Here. I'll buy, you fly." He held out a crumpled five.

"I got it," I said to him. I stretched my back as I stood up next to Gary. "You want a coffee? I'm buying."

His dark eyes were focused elsewhere. "Nah. I gotta go." I watched his lean but still muscular body, covered only by faded overalls, and wearing sandals, lope off in the direction of Avenue B.

Climbing back into my seat with the coffees, I saw my partner was balancing the clipboard on his knee while he wrote.

"Ohhh. Shit! We got a job?"

"Yeah. Let's go. Jumper down."

He swung out into traffic as I folded a piece of the coffee lid back. We both sipped and swore when hot coffee spilled over the lids as we wove down the street.

I dumped the remainder of the coffee the minute my feet hit the sidewalk. Two medics I recognized were already at the side of the woman whose petite body lay still on the sidewalk, arms spread wide as if offering a hug to all who stopped to stare.

Andreus nodded to me, his dark skin pressing against the sweat-soaked white uniform shirt. "Hey, how ya doin'? We got this one. Go check out upstairs. Lots of yelling and screaming. PD's up there. Second floor, I think." He turned back to the woman, holding her head as his partner gently rolled her onto a long backboard.

I could hear the screams as soon as I entered the unlit hallway. The setting sun offered some light from the small windows at the top of each landing on the narrow wooden stairs. An officer peered over the railing on the third floor. He was tall and skinny, with red hair sticking to the sweat on his forehead. His ears were pressed forward by his new uniform cap. He had been pacing the landing two floors above me, worry lines in his forehead growing deeper with each scream that came from somewhere down the hall.

Climbing up towards him, I asked, "What's going on up here? More than one patient?"

"I-I'm not sure. Nobody speaks English. I think this is the husband up here. N-not sure what's going on."

I reached the third floor in time to see an Asian man run from an open apartment door, screaming words that I assumed were Chinese. He was wearing nothing but cutoff shorts and waving a long black spatula in the air as he ran down the hall. A large cop came out of the doorway next, one hand on his gun belt as he ran after the man.

The red-haired rookie pointed me in the direction of the open door. "Go in there. The k-kids. Stay with them." He did a duck-walk trot down the hall in search of his partner.

The kitchen started just inside the open door, with a stove and a tiny table. Four mismatched wooden chairs were squeezed against the table, which was cluttered with unopened mail, a stained chopping block, and an open box of Cheerios. A single light bulb was burning dimly on a wire that hung from a water-stained ceiling.

A film of grease gave the whole kitchen the look of an out-of-focus, sepia-stained photograph. It smelled of used cooking oil.

I had to turn sideways to enter with my trauma bag and made my way down the short, narrow walkway past a sleeping area covered by a privacy curtain and out into what passed for a living room. Two girls, maybe four and five years old, were huddled together on a torn loveseat that took up most of the space. They were sobbing loudly and stared as I squeezed around a wicker basket filled with unfolded laundry. I put down my bag, unsure what to do next. I moved past a cluttered desk to peer out the open window at the crew lifting the stretcher into the ambulance thirty feet below.

A bent window screen lay on the floor under the window. I tried to block out thoughts of what the girls might have just witnessed.

I couldn't tell them that everything was okay. The small, still body on the stretcher was probably their mother. The spatula-swinging, screaming man their father? Had he pushed the mother? Had she fallen? Jumped? I looked again out the window. The man in the shorts, whom I assumed was the father, was being helped into the back of the squad car.

Wait! You can't leave! Who's taking the kids? Who is taking care of these kids? My panicking mind raced with questions. I looked back at the girls. All of my training and experience were worthless in fixing the horror that was unfolding in their young lives.

My partner was down there on the street, talking to the other cop, who then turned, climbed in the driver's seat, and drove off towards First Avenue, following the ambulance to Bellevue.

I turned again to the girls, who by then were shaking, their eyes red and swollen. "What's your names?" They only cried louder. "Do you speak English?" I got no response except more sobbing.

I found a small address book on the desk. A thick rubber band held the pages inside the metallic red cover, an ornate dragon wrapping around from front to back. I slowly turned the pages, dismayed that all the names were in Chinese characters. The numbers were in English, though—or however one referred to numbers that were recognizable. I randomly chose one of the phone numbers and dialed the phone. No answer. I dialed another one. A female, speaking Chinese, answered. What could I say? I tried speaking English. She continued speaking in Chinese, her lilting small voice getting faster and louder. "I'm sorry."

I hung up and tried a few more numbers. No one understood me.

I heard Frank call from the hallway, "Hey, you in there? We gotta get going. Cops said to bring the kids to the hospital. Let's go."

The girls were crying quietly now, listening to Frank's voice in the distance. They both had bare feet. The younger girl kicked and rubbed hers against the worn fabric; bubble gum-pink nail polish dotted her tiny toes. Her sister held her and rocked back and forth, mouth open and silent in between gasps and sobs. I sat for a moment on the loveseat. They clung to me, and I had no words. My chest and throat filled with grief, my eyes with tears. I lifted them both— one on each hip—and grabbed my trauma bag. We squeezed our way back towards the kitchen.

Smelling the cooking oil again, I bent down to check the stove. A low blue flame was flickering against the black underside of the wok. The girls' arms wrapped tightly around my neck as I leaned down and turned off the flame. It flickered one last time and then went out.

THE SKY WAS DARK WHEN I CARRIED the two girls towards the ER ambulance entrance. As always, it was standing room only in Bellevue's emergency room. The triage nurse stared at me as I approached her desk. "The other medic unit, the one that just brought in the trauma—the um, jumper. These are the kids from the apartment. No relatives around. Cops told us to bring them here."

Her gaze went from one child to the other. A brief expression of pain quickly fled from her face, replaced by a stoic look that I could have easily mistaken for anger. "Wait here a second. I'll be right back."

The older girl was sucking on her fingers and leaned her head against my shoulder. Both girls clung to small fistfuls of my uniform shirt.

Looking down at a chart, the triage nurse seemed distracted as she came back to the desk. "Take them down to Social Services." A well-manicured hand gestured towards a long hallway.

"Social Services? And then what?" I looked at her, hoping that she had a better plan. Was I just supposed to leave the two kids there and walk away?

"Someone there will take them. They have to be processed."

"No family members are here? What about—you know. Is she okay?" I avoided saying mom, figuring it would start the girls crying all over again.

This time the nurse, *Frazer* the nameplate read, looked at me. Her eyelashes were long and curly, dark brown against her blue eyes. A small, wet line of mascara was slowly moving down her cheek. She quickly brushed it into a dark smudge, wiping it across her cheekbone. Moving her hand slightly from her face, she just pointed in the direction of the hallway. "Down the hall. On the left." Her voice was small and she turned away, picking up another chart, and loudly calling out to the crowd, "Jenkins? Mr. Jenkins? Over here. You're next. Have a seat."

I made my way down the hallway, where large olive green tiles alternated with off-white and gold-speckled ones. I tried to stay in the green tiles only, and I avoided stepping on the cracks. The ER noise became a distant hum as I passed office doors, most of them closed for the night. The girls were quiet. I could feel their stares.

A doorway ahead spilled light onto the tiled floor. The blending harmony of Crosby, Stills, and Nash slowly moved across the stillness.

At first I thought the office was empty. Two metal-framed couches with orange plastic cushions were pushed against one wall. Three folding chairs lined another. A single small table had New Yorker magazines hastily arranged along with a few High-lights for Children. I could see what looked like a small office in the back, a brighter light on in there, and I tapped on the half-open door. The music abruptly stopped, and a tall, dark-skinned man appeared, his tie-dyed shirt visible through a white lab coat too short in the sleeves. He was a curious mix of Soul and Sixties.

"Uhhh, did the ER call you? These kids, their mom—"

"Yep. Got it. Hey, girls. Come on. Let's go have a seat."

His manner was gentle as he lifted each of the girls from my arms. Placing them in his office, both little bodies in a big black leather swivel chair, he turned to me: "Okay, I got it from here. Thanks."

"That's it? I mean, do you need to sign anything? Do I need to sign anything? Just leave them here?"

"That's it. We'll process everything from here."

I left the office and walked back out to the hall, not paying any more attention to the tiles or the cracks. I felt too light, empty.

The trip back towards the chaos of the ER felt shorter than the journey down. My chest was filled with anguish, and I had more questions than answers.

I climbed back into the passenger seat feeling lost and empty. "You okay?" Frank looked over at me as the ambulance lurched over a speed bump near the exit of the hospital.

"Yeah. Fine. Just. . .man. This really sucks. Those kids. . .." I couldn't say any more.

We drove in silence back down to our post at St. Mark's and Second.

IT'S BEEN ABOUT THIRTY-FIVE YEARS since I let go of those girls in a stark office down the hall from the trauma room where their mother's lifeless body was draped with a plain white sheet.

I think about both of them and wonder what happened. To me, they are still the frightened little sisters on a warm summer evening, bewildered by the sharp turn their lives had just taken. I have prayed for them often and wonder who came for them.

Are they okay? Do they have children of their own? Do they have memories of a night so many years ago when a young paramedic held them and never felt more helpless?

When someone who is curious asks me about the worst call that I've even been to, I think of them. I fall short of speaking about them, though. It wasn't a particularly gory scene. And I didn't treat their mother. It wasn't the worst trauma that I ever witnessed. It was the sadness. Who could understand unless they were there to feel the despair of two little girls? Who would not agree that it was one of the worst calls because I could do nothing to ease the pain?

It's not the blood, or the shock of multiple injuries, or the patients for whom resuscitation efforts are unsuccessful. It's for those who are left behind and the pain that, somehow, sometimes, seeps into our souls that makes the burden heavy. We carry it, wonder about their lives, hope that they're okay.

THE ONLY THING
THAT MATTERS

WHAT IS IT ABOUT CERTAIN MOMENTS in life that we know, when they are happening, they'll stay with us forever? Once in a while something happens—we read or hear words that we think are new and true. What I've come to believe is that we know the truth but need to be reminded sometimes. We recognize this truth, and that re-knowing jolts us somewhere deep inside, where all truths reside.

One experience, unexpected and profoundly simple, has illuminated one such truth for me for decades.

We were called to the scene of "a man down" and found him curled up (as much as one man can curl his body on a narrow bench) in the park. His yellowed, encrusted fingernails seemed to reach out to the empty vodka bottle protruding from a wrinkled brown bag on the ground. A drying puddle of bloody vomit lay next to it.

He pushed himself upright when we called out to him, making only momentary eye contact before looking back down at the bottle and then off into the distance of Tompkins Square Park. "Hi, sir. Did you call the ambulance?" I waited for his answer.

He looked at Frank and me, and shook his head. There were few people in the park on that damp November evening, and I could only assume a passerby had called.

"What's your name?" I asked him.

He sighed quietly. "Robert."

"Well, Robert, how are you feeling? It looks like there's some vomit on the ground, some blood in it. Do you have any pain?" I asked.

Again, he sighed. "No. I'll be fine."

"Robert, we'd like to get you into the back of the ambulance, get your coat off, and take your blood pressure. Check out how you're doing today, okay?"

"I'm fine. No need for all that," he said.

"How about you at least let us check you out," Frank said, "and then we can decide what's best after that? Come on. I'll crank up the heat in the back, and we'll see what's going on."

I covered him with a blanket on the stretcher after we removed a heavy woolen coat that looked like it had been expensive and stylish before layers of malodorous grime had worked themselves into the fabric.

"I have no money, no insurance," Robert told us.

"No problem. You still need to get treatment. No one is going to bill you," I said, thinking, He probably has no address to get mail anyway. Like most of the homeless, or *indigent population* as they were politically referred to, were treated at the city hospitals under what I was told was state money for that purpose. For many, the emergency department was a revolving door of care when chronic illness became a life threat. Once all appeared to be under control, those folks were back out on the street until the next crisis. Care and cure could not walk hand in hand.

We suspected an internal bleed based on his blood pressure and the bloody vomit. Dark, crusted blood dotted his lips and beard stubble. We established an intravenous line after several swipes with alcohol pads to clean, as best as we could, a small area of his arm.

"Robert, we're giving you fluids and some oxygen. You should start to feel a little better."

I sat alongside the stretcher as we drove to the hospital. He seemed not to hear me.

"Robert, how are you feeling now?" I inflated the blood pressure cuff again as I waited for his answer.

Looking at the cuff, then at me, he said, "You know, I wasn't always like this. I mean, I used to be pretty successful. I'm sorry to trouble you with this."

Moving my stethoscope aside, I waited for more, but he was silent. "What happened? I mean, in your life? How did it happen that you're on the street now?"

He continued to stare out of the tiny back windows of the ambulance. I looked out too, at the gray sky and bare trees. I waited.

"A few years back, I was working with a top designer here in the City. You probably heard of him." Robert told me the name of one of the leading fashion designers in the world.

"I was actually one of his partners. Had everything. My beautiful wife and I were expecting our first baby." He stopped talking.

". . .She went into labor early. There were complications. She died. The baby died." He took a breath and was lost again in the dark November sky outside the ambulance windows.

"Oh, that's. . .oh, my God. So awful." My words sounded trite.

Looking back at me, he tilted his head to one side. "You know, there's a lot of stuff that we get caught up with in life. What we think is important. When my wife and the baby died, I just stopped caring. I stopped getting up in the morning. Didn't go to work. Wouldn't answer the phone."

Again, he looked out the window. "Pretty soon I lost everything—my job, my apartment, friends. But it just didn't matter. Nothing mattered."

I was silent, couldn't imagine the depth of his despair.

Breaking his stare out the window, he looked back at me. "You know, there's only one thing in life that matters. And that's to love and be loved."

Somehow, at that moment, on a damp, gray November evening, I knew that I had heard a truth that would illuminate a part of me. And that light, that *reknowing,* has stayed with me, reminding me always of what matters most.

TEA FOR TWO

THERE WAS NO DOORMAN for that building. The dented metal front door of the five-story walkup was propped open with an ancient cracked brick, crumbling mortar still stuck to one side. My partner and I each had about forty pounds of equipment—heart monitor, double oxygen resuscitator, drug box, portable stair chair. The monitor hung from a strap on my shoulder and banged my hip with each step. Actually, we never really weighed all of the equipment, and depending on who you were talking to and what the weather was like and which floor of the building where we had to go, the weight changed. The hotter the day, the more flights we climbed, the heavier we claimed it was. It didn't matter. It was always too heavy when you added a patient to the chair and some sense of urgency.

The inside of the building was thick with summer humidity, though it was shaded from the sun. Dark stains in the corner by the stairway promised to be old urine, judging from the dank smell that mingled with the aroma of curry drifting from one of the closed apartment doors.

Frank stopped at the bottom of the stairs and placed the drug box down to free one of his hands. Wiping sweat from his forehead, he asked, "What floor again?"

I gave him a stare. *The* stare. "Fifth. Of course. Came over as a sick."

He chuckled. "Yep. Ninety-eight degrees. No elevator. Fifth floor. Of course. And who *wouldn't* be sick in this place? You know, they don't even *allow* air conditioners here? They say it's not wired for it. The building is—I don't know, like a hundred years old? Maybe more. Probably like an oven up there."

It was still early in our three-to-eleven shift. Mid-July, and certain to be a busy night.

We were silent and breathing hard by the time we

found apartment 5-C. I lifted and dropped the handle of an old- fashioned brass knocker on the door and waited. After about a minute I gave it two more sharp taps. "Paramedics!" I waited.

A chain rattled, several locks turned, and the door slowly opened. A small woman with a thinning head of white hair and thick glasses peered around it. Her white-and-lavender flowered housedress hung limp, at least four sizes too big.

"Come in. Come in." She turned faster than what I expected from such a frail body and was already making her way into a tiny kitchen. We followed.

A white Formica table the size of a card table sat in the center of the kitchen. Four metal chairs with thin cushions were pushed neatly under it. "Please. Sit down." She gestured to the chairs and smiled.

"Ma'am, did you call the ambulance today?" Frank asked, looking around the kitchen and trying to see the rest of the apartment. "Is anyone else here? Is the ambulance for you?"

"Well, yes. Please, sit." Again she looked at the chairs.

I placed the heart monitor on the floor and the airway bag on the chair. Opening it, I took out the blood pressure cuff.

Smiling, she said, "Oh, I don't think I need any of that."

"Ma'am, what seems to be the problem today?" Frank asked again, and smiled. "Are you sick? Do you have any pain? Any trouble breathing?"

"Well, no. Not really. I just. . . ." She stared off. "Would you like some tea?"

Frank caught on before me. He chuckled and asked her, "You wanted to have tea with someone, so you called 9-1-1?"

For just a second I saw fear, sadness, panic, and shame on her face. She said nothing, but looked down at the table. "Maybe I *was* feeling a little bit sick. Or maybe it was just my nerves. It's just me here. My husband is dead. My son died two years ago. My daughter lives in Michigan. She's doing quite well. She's a school teacher, you know."

Frank and I looked at each other. I tried to hide my impatient sigh.

"At least let me take your blood pressure," I said.

She sat and lifted a shaking arm, and I gently wrapped the blood pressure cuff over her papery thin skin.

"I'm very healthy. I don't want to trouble you. And I certainly don't want my daughter knowing about this. She'll have me move out there with her. I don't want to be any bother for anyone." She watched the needle on the blood pressure gauge bounce down the numbers as she spoke.

"Blood pressure is great," I told her.

"You're very kind. At least let me put on the kettle and get you some tea."

Frank started packing up the equipment. "I'll take this down to the bus and get on the radio. Make us available. I don't know—I guess we make this an RMA?"

I thought for a moment. "She isn't really refusing medical aid. Just doesn't have any complaints," I said.

Frank took out the ambulance call report that was rolled up in his back pocket. "Ma'am, do you want to go the hospital?"

"Heavens, no!" She looked from me to Frank and then back at me. "Of course not!"

"Okay. Just sign here. There you go. RMA." Frank rolled up the sheet and stuffed it back into his pocket. "My partner here will have some tea with you, and I'll bring this stuff back to the ambulance. You have a nice night."

I looked at Frank. He smiled and said, "Well, you're already sitting. I'll let the dispatcher know we're available. I'll call you on the portable if we get a job." And he was gone.

Our patient or not-patient, I don't recall her name, looked happy. The flame was on full beneath the old aluminum teapot. She placed china tea cups and saucers on the table. The cups had roses painted on them inside and out. Faded gold circled the fluted rims. Placing a chipped but matching sugar bowl on the table, she asked, "Do you take milk?"

"Uh, sure. Milk and sugar. Great." I felt awkward and clumsy in my heavy uniform pants and black boots. My shirt was sticking to my back.

She poured the hot water over the tea bags in the cups with surprising ease and then shuffled slowly across the kitchen to place the kettle back on the stove.

We sat and talked about life. She told me about her family, her life in New York City for so many decades in a time that I could only imagine.

When it was time to leave, I felt somehow that she had done more for me than I for her. She thanked me for staying, again assuring me that she felt fine and that she must have been "just a little nervous" when she called.

"So how was your tea?" Frank asked.

"Fine. Weird. What *was* that, anyway?" I shook my head and we headed out to finish the shift.

WHY ARE SOME AMBULANCE CALLS more memorable even after thirty-five years? Why did that elderly woman call 9-1-1 for a vague medical condition when, really, she just wanted someone to sit and have tea with her? I'm still not sure what the purpose was for me being there. Or why we didn't get any ambulance calls for the thirty or forty minutes that we were there when, by all rights, we should have. It was hot. It was humid—a late afternoon on Manhattan's Lower East Side. Yet the world, for that small wedge of time, was quiet. Was the universe conspiring to teach me a lesson? Was I overthinking the whole event?

Perhaps it was just the way things worked out that day. That I should say yes to something unexpected. When we do that, we are really saying yes to the gifts that we so often overlook each day. When we stop and notice a bird splashing in a puddle, we are accepting a simple and joyous gift of that moment. When we learn that bending to smell a newly blossomed rose really is the world's way of slowing us down, forcing us to bend and exhale before we deeply inhale the fragrance of a flower, we accept a gift of that moment.

For most of us, somewhere between childhood and old age, we lose our sense, not just our senses.

When we take out the garbage at night, do we stop for just a few seconds to turn our heads up to see the stars and maybe, by chance, see a shooting star or a lone cloud drifting, illuminated in front of the moon?

What does it cost us to slow down and see all that the world offers?

I surprised myself by actually enjoying that cup of tea with an elderly stranger. Our paths crossed for just a short time, but I remember that day and how I sat in her kitchen on an old metal chair, restless at first that I would have to run out to a call. But all remained still. Was it some profound lesson? Or was it more simple—that no one should ever have to have tea alone every single day?

TEACHER

I MET WALTER ONLY ONCE. Thirty-five years ago, my paramedic partner, Frank, and I responded to a call for a "man down in the hallway" of one of the then-many run-down tenements in Manhattan's Lower East Side. On the first landing of the stairs inside the building, a dark shape was curled into a fetal position. His outer layer was a heavy dark wool coat. The cuffs of two or three sweatshirts in various stages of raggedness were pulled down from the coat sleeves and over his reddened, rough hands.

I placed my medication bag and EKG monitor off to the side of his still body and called out to him. "Hey. Hey! Can you hear me? Are you okay?" Squatting down partway, but far enough from swinging distance, I firmly tapped his shoulder. Even before his eyes opened, his hands responded by seizing the grimy backpack that was secured to his body with twine.

His eyes opened as he slowly pushed himself to a seated position. Stretching his legs out to the first step, he looked at my uniform, then up at me, and he smiled. "What can I do for ya, darlin'?"

Wait. What? He's sleeping in a stairwell, clearly filthy with his worldly possessions fitting in one small pack, and he wants to know what he can do for me? This was not the response I expected. "Someone called us. They saw you here and figured you were unconscious, so we're here to see if you're okay. What happened to your lip?" I'd noticed some dried blood and a suture-worthy split at the corner of his lower lip.

He touched his mouth and looked at his hand before replying, "Well, I guess I'm just pretty fine. No complaints, except that you woke me up."

"What happened to your lip?" I asked him.

"Just defendin' my property. Everything I own, right here." He patted the pack tied to his waist.

"You need a couple of stitches in your lip," I told him.

Again the smile. "I'll be fine."

"And don't keep smiling, or your lip will open up again and start bleeding."

"I always smile. Life is good. And I have this angel taking care of me. Why not smile? You're a nurse?" He looked at my partner and winked.

"No. A paramedic. And we need to take you to the hospital to get your lip stitched up. If you leave it, you'll have a scar and maybe get an infection." I did my best to persuade him to come with us.

"You'll ride in the back with me?"

"Yes, I'll be with you." After a quick exam to rule out any other injury or acute illness, I helped him to his feet, and we walked out to the ambulance. I asked the basic information. His name was Walter.

"So, Walter, why sleep on the stairs? Why not get a bed at the shelter over on Third?" I had been inside the men's shelter at Eight East Third Street. Back in those days, it housed hundreds. Dozens more homeless, addicts, emotionally disturbed, and other lost souls spilled out onto the sidewalk and nearby doorways. Inside, it stank. It was dark and depressing. The rooms were tiny, if one was lucky enough to get one; each had a small bed, a tiny nightstand/dresser, a single lightbulb with a string, and a door—unlike the "Big Room" that contained row after row of metal cots with flimsy mattresses. All residents used the foul-smelling bathroom. For showers, they were bussed elsewhere.

As if reading my thoughts, he replied, "Have you been there? I'm safer out here on the street. I got my warm coat and a few other things here in my pack. Nobody's taking my stuff from me."

As we made a slow trip to the hospital, I convinced him to untie his pack before covering him with two warm blankets.

"So, Walter, are you from the City originally?" It was my way of striking up a conversation about something other than medical matters, a way to help some of the homeless recall dignity or at least engage in some regular conversation.

"Ohhhh, no. I'm from Upstate. Sullivan County. My family had a dairy farm. After my parents died, they left me the farm but, you know, times are bad. Bank took it. Most everybody in our town. . .used to have us lots of farms. Dairy, cattle. A regular ghost town now, it is." Walter stared ahead, and his face fell into an expression of memories for a moment. He quickly shook off whatever far-away thoughts were there. "But you know, I'm okay. I came to New York City with nothing. Lost it all after the bank took away my farm. But I made it. I been livin' here on the street for two years. And if I can make it here, I can make it anywhere, right?" He did the smile thing again. And he truly looked okay—except for the oozing cut on his lip.

"You have no family? No sisters, brothers?" I asked.

"Nope. Just me." He watched me as I thought about his response.

"Huh," was all I said, and thought, *What if I had no more family? No job? No savings? What if the bank just came one day and auctioned off the only home I had ever known? All of my neighbors as poor as me. Friends gone.* I couldn't comprehend his life.

Again, as if reading my thoughts, he said, "I'm fine. I'm content out here. I have warm clothes. I know where to get food. Got a couple of good friends. I'm making it."

I knew life on the street was about as hard as it could get in this country. In this city. Half-eaten bagels were fished out of trash baskets. Still-edible food was scored from dumpsters near high-end restaurants. Newspapers doubled as reading material and blankets on a park bench at night. Showers were rare, public toilets nonexistent. And yet. . .Walter was grateful for his clothing, for food, and for finding a place to sleep that was safe. He had a social circle.

IN SANSKRIT THERE IS A WORD—so much more than a word—Upa Guru or upaguru. It refers to the person or thing next to you that becomes your teacher. Ram Das reminds us that the Upa Guru, "anyone and everyone who crosses our path, has come to teach us something."

Walter and his smile, his rough dairy-farmer-turned-street-survivor hands pulling his old wool coat around his curled-up body, was just one of many people that I've met—survivors, homeless people (not The Homeless), people who by choice or circumstance, through addiction or psychiatric malady, knew the other side of There But For Fortune—who have shaped my life.

I am grateful for lessons of Walter and others who struggled to survive. He was likely an exception rather than the rule of those on the street. Was he truly happy? It is not for me to know.

So often, in the past thirty-plus years, when I pull a warm blanket up to my chin, my head resting on a clean pillow with a small cool breeze blowing in a window that I can close if I need to. . .I feel thankful.

HELLO
AND GOODBYE

THE BROAD-CHESTED POLICE OFFICER standing near the partially opened door was tall. He heaved an audible sigh of relief when he saw me. "Oh, thank God. A female." He stepped out of his sentry-at-the-door position and gestured us to come in. Looking at my partner, he rolled his eyes. "This is bad. This woman is. . .well, you'll see."

He looked back at me and then said to my partner, "Let her go in. I'll give you the information in the living room. The husband is in there. The lady—a miscarriage, I think. We covered it, in a pail. The husband doesn't want her to see it."

The guys walked into the living room. I tapped

gently on the bedroom door and pushed it the rest of the way open. "Hi. I'm Gail, a paramedic." I took a deep breath and entered, not sure what to say next.

The woman, in her late twenties I figured, was sitting on the edge of her bed, crying, and had a towel draped over her lap. Trying to speak, she moved the towel, revealing blood on the inside of her thighs. Then she pointed to a pail near the door. "I want to see my baby." Her voice was quiet, pleading.

I lifted the towel from the pail to inspect. The small body, with fully formed arms, legs, genitalia, and a sweet, gentle face, lay curled and motionless. The attached umbilical cord and placenta in a bloody heap beside it. I had no doubt that a resuscitation was not necessary. Replacing the towel, I walked back over to the woman and moved a wooden chair over in front of her. I sat silently for a moment. Again, sobbing quietly, she said, "Please. I just want to see my baby, hold him. Can you tell? Is it a boy or a girl?"

"It's a boy," I said.

She nodded as if she knew.

"We can do that. First, please let me make sure you're okay." I held her wrist and measured her pulse. It was fast but strong. Her blood pressure reading alleviated my fear of extensive blood loss. I asked her to move the sanitary pad aside and examined her for any heavy bleeding. "I'll have to take you and the baby to the hospital. You probably won't need to stay too long, but—just to make sure everything is okay."

She nodded and waited.

I opened two packages of twelve-by-thirty-inch sterile trauma dressings and gently wrapped the fetus—the baby—her son, inside them. I tucked the placenta behind him, wrapped out of view. Just his face was visible when I handed the tiny bundle to her.

She caressed his face and then unwrapped the trauma dressing just enough to touch each tiny finger. "I knew you would understand." She looked at me with a sad smile. "Do you have children?"

"I don't."

We sat for a few more minutes.

THE POLICE OFFICERS and her husband looked confused but said nothing when they saw her holding the baby. She held him even as she was buckled into the stretcher; and she held him all the way to the hospital.

I wrote up my paperwork and estimated the fetus—her son—to be about four to five months gestation. She had no other children. As I wrote, I wondered what plans she had had for that child. Who would he have looked like? What talents would he have shown as he grew up?

I tried not to judge the police officers or her husband. They could not understand the intimacy that had already developed between mother and child. I couldn't either, having no children of my own. Almost ten years later, I would know what it was like to have tiny feet push ripples into my belly and feel the kicks and flips when my daughters danced through amniotic fluid long before they took their first breaths. I knew them well even before I saw their beautiful faces, held their tiny fingers.

Looking back, I'm glad and grateful that I was witness to her lovingly holding a baby who had never taken his first breath. The father rode with us and eventually looked at his son's face and cried. I want to believe that, together, they healed, that they had healthy children in the years that followed.

There was something beyond words that day. It's not about pro-life or pro-choice or at what age a fetus becomes a baby or a person. It was simply standing back and allowing life to take its course. It was about allowing a young mother and father—and they *were* parents at that moment—to acknowledge the person whose life they had dreamed about, whose small squirms and kicks they had touched each night through her growing belly.

For them, it was a chance to say hello, and a chance to say goodbye.

HEARING
THE TRUTH

LARKIN, YOU'LL BE RIDING with a new medic today. George. He's had some experience, not too much. Frank is out, so he's your partner for tonight." Tony, my supervisor, had surprised me with this news as I was getting my gear together for the three-to-eleven shift out of Cabrini.

I rolled my eyes. "Where's Frank?"

"Out. You can work with the new guy." He walked back to his office, holding his hand up with his back turned to me, warning me not to complain.

George thrust his hand towards me. He was an in-your-face kind of guy. Not bad looking. Nice cologne and a cool earring (just one—that was the cool thing back then).

He called me *sista*. I held back the urge to roll my eyes again. I wanted to give the shift a chance. I resigned myself to a night of teaching the rookie the ropes of the Lower East Side. With my hotshot attitude, we rolled out.

About twenty minutes into our shift, we received our first call. It was a weekday and still mid-afternoon. The call came over as a school bus accident on the West Side.

I drove, of course, needing to be in control and being the senior medic and all. The traffic was thick, and I wove in and out of it, making the ambulance a part of my body as I floated it through spaces just inches wider than the vehicle.

At Seventh Avenue and Greenwich, as I recall, we found a small bus in the intersection. As we were moving towards it, a woman got out of the bus and approached us.

"I'm the teacher. We have fifteen children—middle school age. I don't think anyone is too seriously hurt, but you'll have to check. They're banged up a bit and really upset."

"Okay. We'll check it out." I turned to George. "Let's see how many injuries we have before we call for additional units. Maybe no one needs to go to the hospital."

Never breaking eye contact with me, George nodded. "Okay. Let's do this, sista."

The teacher turned to us as we carried our equipment over to the bus. "Oh, one more thing—all of the children are deaf. I'll translate as best as I can, but they're pretty upset right now."

I stopped. "Deaf?" *Oh no,* I thought. *How are we going to do this?* I immediately regretted having a new medic with me and took a deep breath.

George said, "Oh. Okay. No problem. Do they sign?"

"Yes, of course," the teacher replied.

"American or International?" George looked at her intently.

"ASL," she replied.

He nodded as I stood there speechless. *Who is this guy?* I stared at him as his hands began to flip fast and furious, and the kids calmed down one by one.

It turned out that they were more upset than hurt. I think we transported only a couple of them.

Once we were back inside the ambulance, the signing with the injured children continued and George simultaneously voiced the conversation to a very quiet me.

How is it that the universe can so quickly knock us on our ass when we are *acting* like one? There I was, peeved that I had to work with a new guy but resigned to making the best of it. *Be kind, be patient, help him get used to the area, gain his confidence.* Yeah. No, not today.

That was the only time I ever had several hearing-impaired patients. It was my first call with George, who had been born to deaf parents, so signing was his first language. I have not had a call like that since.

Since he had been raised in a household where signing was the primary language, I understood then why he was an "in your face" kind of guy—intense, he never broke eye contact while speaking, always ready to have an open, communicative conversation. Wow.

He never needed my help with any of his skills either. He was (and still is) a top-notch paramedic. He's taught in foreign countries and established programs where none existed.

Sometimes the universe whispers a quiet lesson just when we need it. And sometimes it shouts those lessons at us, and we hear them loud and clear even when they're silent.

LUCILLE

I LIFTED MY CONTAINER of freshly ground peanut butter from the stand under the grinder. The food co-op on the Lower East Side was my favorite place for dinner.

Small chunks of peanuts were floating on top of the warm mixture like pebbles in molten lava. I balanced the plastic container between my arm and my side as I filled a small bag with dates from a pale wooden crate. Next to the crate stood a smaller bin filled with cinnamon sticks, and I inhaled the warm, spicy scent. Moving down the row, my work boots crunched softly against the sawdust on the wide-planked wood floor.

Just as I placed the Medjool dates on the scale in

front of a bearded clerk, I heard the ambulance siren yelp twice. I took a deep breath, paid my bill, and walked quickly out the door while my stomach moved closer to my spine and grumbled about it. I knew better than to buy food that would go bad and, climbing into the ambulance, I quickly stuffed my mouth with a couple of the sweet dates.

Frank was looking at me, a grin on his face. "A seizure. Guess where?"

"Oh, man. Why does she do this? If I don't eat soon, I'm gonna pass out. Want a date?" I stuffed a third one into my mouth, sure that food would hold me for at least another hour, when our shift ended.

Eleven Young, what's your ETA to St. Mark's and Second? You have another call on that seizure.

We were only four blocks from the call. On most nights we'd have been right there at our assigned post. That night, we had taken a detour to the food co-op after we dropped off our last patient at the hospital.

We tried to be enthusiastic about the call, but we were pretty sure who it was. It was Saturday. Out-of-towners. Best audience. Lucille deserved an Oscar for her ability to convince the Weekend Crowd of her sudden and serious seizure activity in the middle of

Second Avenue. Lucille's long black curls and flawless olive skin, which stretched around a slender adolescent body, belied her forty-five years—most of them kind to that body but not so much to her mind. Her body intact, though, she could control crowds of those who didn't know her with her seizures and amnesia and a sudden need for a ride to the hospital, just at our change of tour on Saturday nights.

Kneeling on the side of the road, I leaned down and whispered so the crowd couldn't hear my words, "Lucille. Luuu-*cille*. C'mon. Get up." Her eyelids fluttered at hummingbird speed. No response. "Please. Get. Up. C'mon. Me and Frank will give you a ride home. Let's go."

I caught the glare of a woman—probably from Connecticut, in leather loafers, sweater casually tied around her lime green Izod shirt. She watched. Her eyes narrowed. Probably cursing me to the pits of hell for my callousness and lack of empathy.

But I *did* have empathy. Frank and I were *friends* with Lucille. We'd bought her white leather fringed moccasins for her birthday, the exact ones that she told us about—several times—in a shop window in the West Village in the weeks leading up to her big day.

She had danced around the ambulance that night

after ripping open the package, delighted and carefree as a five-year-old, oblivious to everyone else passing by on that hot July night.

Over the course of the few years that we worked the Lower East Side, she spent hours telling us her life story as her tongue poked through the spaces where her front teeth used to be.

I thought about this as I lowered my head again to her ear. "Lucille. Please. Get up." We were definitely not lacking in empathy. It's just that we wanted her to get off the street, so that we could call it a night.

Sometimes our pleading worked. Sometimes. . . well, not this night. We knew that the only way we would get back for change of shift was to take her with us.

By then, we were over being annoyed. Trying to hold my mouth in a straight line and hide the urge to grin, we lifted her onto the stretcher and pulled the straps snug.

The glaring Izod-wearing woman seemed satisfied and pumped her loafers down the sidewalk, not glancing back.

I spoke to Lucille in my normal tone, as if she were a friend sitting next to me on the bus and not someone in the throes of some wild, prolonged seizure activity.

A few blocks from the hospital, her eyelids fluttered a few more times, and she opened her eyes and mumbled, "Whahh happened? Where am I?"

"You're in the ambulance, Lucille. You had a seizure. Where's April? Where's your dog?"

"Ummm. I took her home before," she said in her quiet, childlike voice. "I'm sorrrry. I didn't mean to have a seizure. I just don't want you guys to go home. Can't you stay and work a little longer?"

"Lucille, we can't. Come on. We're at the hospital. Let's go."

"What are you and Frankie doing after work? Can I go with you? Are you going out?"

"We have a party. With the nurses from the ER."

"Can I come? Please? Please?"

Frank was standing in the open door. "Come on, Lucille. Time to go."

She twirled a long black banana curl in her grubby hand. The ER bay lights glittered in her teary eyes. "Please?" Her lower lip quivered.

"Okay. Fine. You can go. We're meeting at the place next door to the Crabhouse, around the block. Wait here for us."

Her small feet danced down the ambulance steps to the sidewalk. Skipping around the ambulance, her

GAIL LARKIN

white moccasins made small shussings against the concrete. "I'll wait right here!"

"ARE YOU GUYS KIDDING?" Violet, the head nurse watched as Frank and I walked into the party with Lucille happily alongside us. "Really?"

"Oh, she'll be fine. Right, Lucille?" Frank chuckled and ordered her a soda.

That's how it went back then. You spent so much time on the street that the lines between patients and friends sometimes blurred. I think every crew had their regulars. Sometimes it just made you think about life differently.

On some nights we were so busy with back-to-back calls that there was just no wait time between them. The dispatcher would call us on the radio the moment we came back after dropping off a patient in the ER.

One-one-young, I'm holding several jobs. Got a man down, possible cardiac arrest. Fourteenth and Second. An overdose—two-two-two East Two. Confirmed. Another—possible jumper up. First Avenue between Twenty-sixth and Twenty-seventh. What's your ETA to the closest?

Other nights, we finished cups of coffee, built up piles of sunflower seed shells outside our ambulance window, had long conversations with people who lived on the street or were regulars. These were the nights that Lucille would tell us the stories of her life.

At some point, a bond developed. Burn-out and PTSD are not the only dangers of working on the street. Getting close to people—people whom you otherwise would never have maybe known, maybe people that you would have avoided in school or in your neighborhood, was another danger, or risk, depending on how you looked at it.

You find yourself thinking about them, looking forward to seeing them on your shift, hearing their stories, true or not.

Lucille loved to dance, and she did so without a shred of self-consciousness on the corner of Saint Marks and Second. She danced like a child in front of her parents and then giggled and skipped back to the open ambulance window.

There is a joy and a simplicity in life that so often slips away as we get down to the business of living. I think it's the erosion of spontaneity that steals happiness. And the very act of trying to plan out happiness is what keeps it from being.

If only we could dance with abandon and tell friends that we just want to visit with them, without worrying about judgment and rejection. She usually wanted nothing but a bit of our time and company (and the occasional birthday present!).

She invited me into her apartment one time. Her bathtub was filled with plaster from a collapsed ceiling above it. She had a small folding table and a few folding chairs. Not much more.

Somewhere in her apartment she had a bonnet-style hairdryer that Frank and I had given her one year (she insisted that was all she needed, and loved to dry her curlered hair the old-fashioned way). She also had watercolor paints and loved making paintings but probably loved giving them away even more.

How is it that some people become avatars of the elusive parts of life? She is Lucille, but she is also Joy, Spontaneity, Honesty. Decades later, from a distance, I can see all of it so much more clearly.

Somewhere in my attic, I still have her paintings.

SOCKS

THE GLARE OF THE RISING SUN reflecting off the windows of surrounding hi-rises created an illusion of warmth on that frigid January day. I was doing an extra shift before my usual three-to-eleven-p.m. tour, and I had prepared accordingly.

Before leaving for the drive from Staten Island to work that morning, I'd stuffed my backpack with the usual supplies for my shift—granola bars, book, protocols, peanut butter-and-jelly sandwich, Swiss Army knife, dental floss, a change of clothes in case there was anything going on after work. I threw in a few extra snacks for the double shift, and then, as an afterthought, I grabbed a pair of new woolen ski socks.

Socks weren't usually on my grab-and-stuff list

when I was filling my backpack for work. It was a random addition and one that I had never made before, or made since, that day.

"So this is how we roll on the day shift." I think my partner that day was a paramedic named Jimmy. He wasn't my usual partner, but he was eager to set me straight on how things were done on the "Seven A" shift, seven a.m. until three p.m.

"First thing, before we do anything. Coffee. Breakfast. Egg and cheese on a roll from a place over on First." He drove slowly through the empty Manhattan streets on that cold, clear Sunday morning.

"Fine with me." I was already tossing a handful of sunflower seeds into my mouth in an attempt to quiet my grumbling stomach. "I'm starving. And I definitely need coffee."

We parked on a sunny corner just a few blocks from the hospital. The radio was blessedly quiet. We tucked the brown paper under our egg sandwiches and ate in silence.

Jimmy gulped his coffee after tossing the greasy papers in the garbage between our seats. "You know," he said as he picked a particle of roll or cheese from his tooth, "Sundays are usually pretty good. No calls till maybe—ohhh. Here we go." He looked past me to the sidewalk. "Maybe we got ourselves our first customer."

A man, wearing an oversized coat with one button fastened, was walking slowly towards us, his feet barely rising off the ground with each step. There was no one else around. His coat flapped in the bitter wind, and as he moved closer I could see his red-rimmed eyes were watery. Anyone living on the street in such a season was, to me, a hardy soul, no matter how hopeless or ill they were. As he approached the ambulance, I rolled down the window. Icy air blasted its way into the warm cab.

"I'm—I'm sorry to bother you guys. Do you know where I can get a hot shower? I just need a shower."

His face spoke of needs so much vaster than that. Malnutrition and poor sleep have a way of casting themselves into the characteristics of the face. Red, rough cheeks, tiny broken blood vessels across his nose, cracked lips with sores at the corners: Poor nutrition, exposure to the heat and rain and sleet, and most likely a daily consumption of cheap alcohol had etched a look onto his face and demeanor that was impossible to fake.

"If you go over to Cabrini and see Violet, the head nurse in the ER, she'll fix you up. There's a shower room there, and she can get you some clean clothes, too." *And probably a lice treatment while she's at it*, I thought.

It was typical for people living on the street to have a number of chronic illnesses. Lice and scabies were common. In those days, Cabrini Hospital had a stainless-steel-and-tile shower room where clothes were stripped off and the homeless were shaved, scrubbed, fed, and then examined. It took an enormous amount of the nurses' time and patience, but most of them accepted it as part of their job in the emergency room.

The man, whose name I never did get, thanked us and started to walk away. I felt awful. And guilty. "Do you want some food or something?"

"Nah. Just a shower." He turned again and started walking, and then stopped. Taking the few steps back to the ambulance, he waited while I rolled down the window again.

His shaking fingers, protruding from torn gloves, struggled to grasp the fabric of his pant legs. He pulled the fabric up just enough to uncover his old shoes and purple, swollen ankles.

"Do you think they have any socks there?"

I stared at his ankles for a moment and then asked

him, "Do they have *what?*"

"Socks. Any *socks*. My feet are cold."

"Wait a second." I grabbed my pack and dug for the woolen ski socks that I had stuffed in there earlier that morning. "Here." I held them out the window.

He smiled and pushed the socks into his pocket. "Thanks."

I'D NEVER PACKED SOCKS BEFORE. Never had anyone ask for socks before. Sometimes, if we allow God, or the Universe, or whatever you believe that small but true voice inside to be. . . sometimes, if we listen, we can encounter miracles.

SMALLEST GIFTS

M OST OF US LOVE GETTING GIFTS. Christmas. Birthdays. Grab-bags at parties. We adore special surprises. I think it's just part our humanness that, when we receive a present, it lifts our mood, arrests our thoughts of yesterday or tomorrow, and pulls us into the present moment.

I've come to realize that the most cherished gifts are those that are small and easily missed if we get too caught up in the busyness of living.

WE RESPONDED TO A CALL for an injury down at the Ninth Precinct, on Fifth Street, in Manhattan. We were on friendly terms with the officers there, and we nodded our hellos as we walked in.

An officer waved us over to a chair where a very tall, slender man in too-short pants was slumped.

"This is Lawrence. He came in to make a report. Someone took his boots. But he has these cuts. Maybe you guys could get him checked out?" The officer pointed to the wounds on the man's face.

"Hey. How ya' doing? What happened?" I placed my equipment on the floor and leaned over to take a closer look at his injuries.

"I don't need no ambulance. I just want my damn *boots* back!" He pointed to his bare feet and started crying. "I just want ma damn boots! Just got 'em." As he cried and talked, his lip started bleeding again. It was clear that he needed stitches.

"What kind of boots were they?" I asked, trying to make conversation.

"Nice boots. Nice leather boots. A guy gave em' to me." In frustration, he again pointed to his bare feet and then let his arm drop to his lap. "I got no place. Nowhere to live. Gotta have shoes. I can't be going around without shoes. It's gettin' cold out." His swiped away the blood and snot from his nose with a large hand.

"Well, look. How about you let us clean up your cuts and take you to the hospital? Maybe we can find you some shoes." I was thinking about what we referred to as the "clothes closet" at the hospital. In addition to the shower room, Cabrini had a closet solely for donations for the homeless population and those who needed fresh clothes, especially after coming into the emergency department with scabies and lice, and clothing caked with old dried feces and street grit.

The nurses sometimes complained, but deep down I believe that they were rightfully proud of the way they so often helped people in need: giving baths, shaving, dumping the old clothes and dressing the folks in used but clean ones. Every mealtime, a big steel rolling cart of sandwiches and juice appeared in the ER. It seemed that sandwiches were handed out more often than Band-Aids.

"WE CAN PROBABLY GET YOU some shoes at the hospital," I told Lawrence as we wheeled his large, lanky frame along in our stair chair.

He stared at me when we were loading him onto the stretcher in the back of the ambulance. "Shoes? You think you're gonna find somethin' to fit me? I got big feet. Ain't gonna be anything for me." He looked at me as if I had suggested we stop and buy a lottery ticket on the way to the hospital.

"Well, we'll see." I said. Maybe there *will* be something there that will fit you."

He tilted his head as if talking to a child. "Honey, I got size fourteen feet. *Now* you think you gonna have somethin' there for me?"

"Oh. Well, who knows?" I doubted that we would but figured it was worth checking the closet.

As soon as I finished giving the patient report to the nurse, I left Lawrence to go check out the clothing closet.

I moved a few bags of clothes, and there, on the floor, was a used pair of black high-top Converse sneakers. There were no other shoes, no other sneakers, not even a slipper in the closet that day.

Yep. Size fourteen. I grabbed them.

Pulling aside the patient privacy curtain, I held up the sneakers. "Lawrence! I have them. Your size!"

I slipped them on his feet, and we both smiled. It was the first of two miraculous gifts from the universe that day.

He looked at his feet. "One of 'em is missing a shoelace."

I suddenly remembered something.

We miss gifts if we don't look up. We miss things if we don't look down. I remembered a shoelace out on the ground by the ambulance bay. A *shoelace*. I remembered having seen it over the past few days, stuck in a little pile of slush. Why had I noticed it? More puzzling, why did I even *remember* it? "Lawrence, wait here. I'll be right back." I hurried outside.

There, exactly where it had been for at least the past two days, was the shoelace. It was white, kind of ratty, and very wet.

I grabbed it as if it were gold.

"Here ya go!" I held up the shoelace. "It doesn't match the other one, but it's long enough for the high tops, and hey, it'll do the trick."

Lawrence smiled as I laced up his other sneaker.

THERE ARE GIFTS IN LIFE EVERY DAY. Most of the important ones are small and easily missed, but these are the gifts that can bring us the most joy.

Imagine wrapping up a shoelace for someone. We can't plan the best gifts. In a truly joyful life, there are no social classes or incomes or price tags.

Joy is about staying in the moment. It's when the Universe (for me, God) carries us along on an effortless current, reminding us that we are neither in charge nor alone.

EVERY ATOM

THE AMBULANCE ROCKED as if on warm ocean surges as we wove through the July afternoon traffic in lower Manhattan. We approached the scene—a pedestrian struck by a truck—at the intersection of Canal and Mott in the middle of Chinatown. The oily pungency of fried rice and dumplings hung heavy in the humidity.

We approached our patient, an elderly, bloodied man, face up and motionless in the street. His eyes were open and blinking at the sky. They didn't leave the sky when I called to him.

One of the cops caught my attention and pointed his chin at the ground. He lifted a white bath towel near the injured man. Underneath the towel was a detached arm, hand purpled and curled upward as if waiting for a gift.

The crowd of Chinese-speaking people created a sort of human hedge along the sidewalk and parked cars. I could hear a few muffled sobs and murmurs, but they were mostly eerily quiet.

The man on the street was small, and it took us only moments to wrap him in a sheet and gently roll him onto a backboard. His left arm was missing. A bloodied stump was partly concealed by his shredded shirt, grit and black drag marks smeared across the pale blue fabric.

Inside the ambulance, I did a more thorough head-to-toe exam, all the while talking to the man although I was certain that he didn't understand English. Large abrasions across his chest were beginning to swell, indicating that the surface wounds, even the amputation, were not his most serious injuries. His slim torso and abdomen were growing more discolored and distended as we made the quick trip to the hospital. His intravenous fluids were running in quickly, but his blood pressure continued to drop. I wished that he could understand my words of comfort.

Just a few blocks more to go and his uninjured arm reached over. His bony hand found mine and squeezed it hard. I was surprised at the strength in such a small person but also in one who was so badly injured. I looked at his face. He stared back. At that moment, something happened that has haunted me for decades.

His eyes were fixed on mine. I thought at first that I saw fear there. Then my perspective changed, and I was him—his thoughts, his emotions. There was no distinction between us. Words cannot capture this, but I'll try. I felt terror. Immediately, my logical self tried to rationalize that he was panicked at the re-alization of what had happened. But I could not keep that connection too long, overwhelmed by something that I have not been able to define for many years.

The man died about an hour later. I felt his ab-sence, yet I've never forgotten that moment, and it has nagged at me as if trying to nudge some lesson or rev-elation into my stubbornness and logic. How could I be him? Was he me? Was there no distinction be-tween us? And why me? For that one moment, I ceased being me and now, so many years later, I real-ize that the terror was my own.

I believe that he was more peaceful than I was with his fatal injuries. But the terror of letting go of self, of ego, was too much for me to comprehend.

When his small fingers curled through mine, we

shared the universe. Walt Whitman wrote, in *Song of Myself*, "for every atom belonging to me as good belongs to you." It would be years before I could truly understand this.

There was no space between us and no time. It was a moment of eternity that scared the shit out of me as I wrestled my hand away and busied it with blood pressure and adjusting the sheet on his body. But he knew. He knew that I saw and understood, and that it would take me decades to realize certain truths.

Now, I still try to understand. I recently read Paulo Coelho's *The Alchemist*. The realization by the boy that all things are one in the spirit of the world helps to make sense of my experience with the dying man. He easily communicated some universal truth in what the Alchemist calls the *universal language*. I guess when it was my time to understand, the tools for understanding appeared.

I sometimes wonder who will hold my hand as I die. Even more, I wonder who will hold it after I die. Who will hold the eternal, vaporous hand and help me find my way from this world to that? I believe there will be many, as it should be. And I will know them. I believe that my patient, whose hand I once held, will be among them.

NO WORDS

D URING MY CAREER, I worked for about a year on an inter-facility transport unit. That meant that we were not in the 911 system but instead responded to calls that came in from other hospitals—mostly small ones in rural areas—for a patient needing transport into the New York City area for specialized treatment. Our specialty was high-risk newborns, pediatrics, and maternity complications.

"Okay, it's the next exit." My partner, Craig, gestured to the road ahead. We had already been driving for two hours. "Another mile or so."

We rolled into town with the windows down, enjoying the smell of cut lawns and warm spring air that rushed in from the quiet streets.

"Make the next right. There." He pointed to a brick building.

"That's it? That's the hospital?" The ambulance bounced over a speed bump. "Where's the emergency room entrance? Man, this is one small operation."

"Small town. Small hospital. Probably one school. One gas station—"

"Ha. Nope. I saw two coming through town," I said.

"There. The sign. *Emergency*." An ambulance was backed in and parked at the entrance.

We got out and stretched. "I guess we'll just leave everything here till we see what we've got?" I hooked the keys onto my belt loop and we walked through the entrance where the automatic double doors swishing open were the only sound.

We were under the impression that we were picking up a child seriously injured in a highway motor vehicle accident.

The attending physician, a tall man with thinning brown hair, had the girl's chart in both hands. His eyes closed as he slowly inhaled and exhaled through his nose, his lips pressed tight. "Doctor Jensen. Erik Jensen." One hand left the chart to shake hands with my partner and with me, returned to it, pressing it possessively against his chest.

"Seven-year-old girl, was one of three people in a car struck head-on by another vehicle on a nearby highway. Came in about four hours ago. . . . She was in the front seat. Belted. The impact was pretty intense. Fractured her hip and pelvis. No major vessel damage. Vital signs are stable. She may need some bone reconstruction. I have her chart and x-rays here. We already had a phone consult with the pediatric orthopedic surgeon who'll be taking over her case in the City."

I was relieved and happy too that the child did not have any apparent or immediately life-threatening injuries. Thank God, an easy transport, I thought.

"She's over there," Jensen said, "on the other side of the nurse's station."

I felt the despair as soon as her eyes met mine. She stared as if she had already asked me a silent question and was waiting for the answer.

Again, Dr. Jensen's breathing was slow and controlled; then he spoke. "As I mentioned, she was belted. In the front seat. The younger sister, five years old, was in the back seat. Also belted. Has some internal injuries. She's in surgery and expected to be okay."

"Okay, so any parent coming with the older sister?" I wondered how a parent would make that decision, whom to leave.

The physician hesitated before speaking again. "We're trying to get in touch with Mom. The daughter says she went shopping and they were spending the day with the father.

'He's. . .he's in bad shape. We were able to get hold of the grandmother. She signed the consent. Someone, a family member, not sure who, will be down at the hospital in the City as soon as possible."

I waited for more details, not sure I wanted more but certain that I would hear them. I was getting the feeling that the source of his stress was about to become way too clear.

"Yeah. Both kids were belted in. They were on the highway. Another car apparently crossed over from oncoming traffic, hit them dead on. The dad wasn't belted in. Went halfway out the windshield. Massive brain injury." He paused. "He's not waking up."

My stomach flipped as I looked across the room at our young patient. "Does she know?"

"No—I mean, we didn't tell her much. Both the kids were conscious when medics found them, though.

They were crying. Dad was unconscious, bleeding from the head. She certainly has some idea."

I could not begin to imagine what those kids felt when the car was hit. Believing that their dad would protect them. And he had, sort of, had made sure that their seat belts were on snug.

I'm guessing that if you ask most parents what their biggest fear, their biggest *nightmare* is, they'd tell you, *losing my child.* But for that little girl, losing a parent in this way is far worse.

As we wheeled her to the ambulance, I could feel her eyes on mine. She needed answers. She would likely never hear her father's voice again. Her mother was still unaware of the horror that had unfolded as she wandered the stores on a beautiful spring Saturday.

The girl's eyes remained on me, and the anguish that I saw in them was far beyond pain that I had ever seen in an adult's eyes.

There was a new burden on the sapling that was her soul. Still green branches, it can bend easily with most burdens. Its limbs will bear what the world places on them and grow thicker, stronger than before. Even years later, when the tree is matured, the burden on that limb will not be hidden from the tree.

She will give that burden on her soul a name. The Day My Father Went Away. She will worry when her younger sister, now moving into her thirties, goes out on a warm spring afternoon. The older sister may wander the mall, worried that another Something Awful might happen. And then she will remember the day her father went away.

We need to give names to the tragedies we accumulate, for to leave them buried and unnamed gives them power beyond our control. Acknowledging these tragedies means that we are able to call upon them to help us love better, be kinder, feel more empathy: Our burden allows us to grow stronger and understand the pain of others.

I don't know anything about that young girl's life now. I can imagine, though, how she might ask friends and loved ones to use a seat belt. "My father was killed in an accident," she might add. But they would not understand the depth and weight of it.

Maybe her own children do not understand why she double- and triple-checks her own seat belt as she drives them to school each morning. Or why she seems so happy, so relieved, when they return from a day out with their dad.

We learn to reach out to others precisely because

we can remember our pain. We call it by different names; yet they each keep us humble and allow us to love more fully, cherish more deeply.

GRATITUDE

I STOOD NEAR THE DOORWAY of the room as my paramedic students arrived for the evening class. One, who already had over ten years on the street as an EMT, was walking slowly.

"Parris, you worked today? You look tired." I could see the weariness in her face and in the slump of her usually squared shoulders.

"Yeah. Yeah, I worked. We had. . .a lot of calls today. We had a child. . . ." She looked away and shook her head. Other younger and less experienced students turned to her as she spoke to me.

"This job. You know, Professor? This job changes you. On the inside." I nodded slowly as she sank onto her seat, opened her notebook.

I knew she would be okay, and that her patients of today, the calls, the stress, would all find their way into her memory and become another part of her life, likely to surface unexpectedly at some time in her far future.

I don't know if it works that way for everybody. What we see, the people we help—in seemingly random fragments of memory, they come back.

Tonight it's raining, a torrential, cold, soaking rain. Save for the brief walk with the dog, I am warm and dry. A cup of hot tea sits within reach. A fragment of memory floats to the surface, a memory from a night quite similar to this, more than three decades back.

WE WERE SOMEWHERE on the Lower East Side, in late fall. A patrol car pulled up alongside the ambulance. The officer in the passenger seat rolled down his window. I did the same. Gusty blasts blew heavy raindrops onto my lap. Shouting above the wind and rain, he said, "There's a guy. Over there." He gestured to the dark, wet sidewalk. "I don't think he's hurt, but he's soaked and just wandering. Maybe you could take him to the hospital? Let him dry out?"

It was a cold rain, the air hovering in the forties,

but the wind made it a much crueler night.

"Well, yeah. Of course." I looked at my partner, who shrugged in agreement. "He'll get hypothermic out here, most likely, if we don't take him in."

I could see a figure, a man, walking slowly along the store fronts, feet shuffling beneath jeans that sloshed about three inches too long through the puddles.

Inside the ambulance, under the bright interior lights, I peeled off his heavy soaked coat and wrapped a blanket around his shoulders.

Momentarily making eye contact, he nodded. "Thank you."

"Are you hungry?" I looked at his gaunt face, the dark stubble on his chin and cheeks.

He nodded.

We stopped on the way in and bought him a sandwich and some juice. He devoured them before we reached the hospital.

It was difficult to work on the street, to see so many people without homes, without hope. It was difficult not to do something from time to time, however small.

Buying him a sandwich was a minute gesture compared to all we had—a good job, homes, families, a future, our health, both physical and mental. Sometimes I wish I had done more, as I'm certain that many of us who worked on the street wish, now that our perspective is clearer.

But it changes you. This job. Every patient, every encounter. Some of the changes are subtle and insignificant. Others, like this man from the rainy night, stay with you. They find a way into your soul like a burrowing microscopic organism waiting quietly, and then suddenly surfacing.

For me, this man and his pain surface on cold rainy nights when the wind beats heavy raindrops against my window and I am warm and dry inside.

Yes, this job, what we carry inside, changes us. I believe it's for the better, though. I am grateful for the smallest things: a hot cup of tea, a place out of the rain, and memories.

I am grateful to those who have given me wisdom in remembering.

EPILOGUE

IN WRITING THIS BOOK over the past two years, so many memories were pulled out of storage. I contacted people that were part of my life—briefly or as steady medic partners or bosses and other EMTs and medics from back in the day.

Some stories were corroborated, and others—well, some were unique to only me, as some of theirs were to them. But after more than four decades, a few things are certain.

First, the job has changed in so many ways. It's no longer the pioneer phase of prehospital emergency medical care in New York City. Equipment is more sophisticated, ambulances more plentiful than ever. Generations of providers have come and gone—some passed simply from old age, some (too many) before their time. On-the-job tragedies such as collisions, accidents, and, of course, 9/11-related illnesses have taken some of the most talented and caring people away too soon. Some EMS providers saw 9/11 as their last day; so many others died, or are dying, from illnesses directly related to their tireless contributions at Ground Zero.

Most of us would not change our choice of careers. New York City Emergency Medical Services is still a relatively new field. The first paramedic class (Jacobi 1!) graduated in 1974. Several members of that class went on to become physicians.

When I graduated from Jacobi (Class 6, 1979), there were only a handful of female paramedics working in New York City. Patients and their families often asked if we were nurses and couldn't comprehend the idea of female paramedics.

Contacting old partners was fun—reminiscing about the old days brought me to the realization that other books needed to be written; new generations of prehospital emergency medical providers should know their roots, especially in two significant aspects of our history.

Firstly, the paths of many of those Jacobi 1 medics

have been impressive and unprecedented. I'm hoping to write or contribute to a book to chronicle those lives.

Secondly, women in EMS were not always so plentiful and accepted. Many are role models and their stories need to be available to all who could learn and follow in their footsteps.

I LEFT THE FIELD for a number of years—raising my daughters, living life. But the call of the siren pulled again like a great magnet, back to the street and eventually, back into teaching EMTs and paramedics, where I am now.

So much has changed in this field, yet one thing will always remain the same. . .

Patients will always be, and they will always need someone to care.

Acknowledgments

I have left out so many stories, left so many colleagues and partners unnamed, ER doctors and nurses (my brother, Jimmy, and my sister, Debby, among them). But I am grateful to them all.

When I walked away from college the first time, back in 1975, I had no idea that my determination to "get out there and live" would venture onto such a long, winding road filled with adventure, heartache, joy, and challenge.

A special thank you to Barry Sheinkopf at The Writing Center, as well as my Wednesday night writing group critics who listened patiently to bits and pieces of this book for two years—Eugenia Koukounas, Ed Dollinger and Edie Messer, Rita Kornfeld, Ora Melamed, Harold Steinbach, Natalie Beaumont, Bill Paladino, and Tony Wiersielis. If I have left anyone out, it's on me.

And thank you to my daughters, Cate and Sarah Minall, and my friends and family members, who tolerated my nagging voice to wear seat belts (and watch out for rip currents!) and who, so many times over the years, insisted that other people would be interested in hearing these stories. I hope they were right.

ABOUT THE AUTHOR

Gail Larkin's career in prehospital emergency care began in 1975 as a volunteer emergency medical technician (EMT). She went on to become a full-time New York City EMT and then a paramedic, stationed at several locations around the city, and taught EMTs and paramedics at the former Health and Hospitals EMS Academy.

She wrote newspaper columns about prehospital medical emergencies for the layperson for twenty-five years, and has contributed to several EMT, AEMT, and paramedic textbooks.

She is currently a full-time professor in a New York City college paramedic program.

Her passion for training future providers lies, not only in helping them learn the theory and skills needed for success, but more importantly, the compassion and kindness that, in her opinion, are the key ingredients in working over the long haul without burning out.

She lives with a very energetic coonhound dog in a New York City suburb.

CPSIA information can be obtained
at www.ICGtesting.com
Printed in the USA
BVHW080050130122
625993BV00011B/1806